W9-CDO-594

EASY BREAD MACHINE BAKING

More than 100 new recipes for sweet and savory loaves and shaped breads

Shirley Ann Holmes, PHEc, BHSc

FIREFLY BOOKS

A FIREFLY BOOK

Published by Firefly Books Ltd. 2000

A Denise Schon/Kirsten Hanson Book
Copyright © 2000 Denise Schon Books Inc.
Text Copyright © Shirley Ann Holmes
Photographs Copyright © Hal Roth

First Printing 2000

Canadian Cataloguing in Publication Data
Holmes, Shirley Ann
  Easy bread machine baking
Includes index.
ISBN 1-55209-493-6
1. Bread. 2. Automatic bread machines. I. Title

TX769.H645 2000   641.8'15   C00-930236-0

U.S. Cataloging in Publication Data
Holmes, Shirley Ann.
  Easy bread machine baking/Shirley Ann Holmes.
  —1st ed.
[160] p. : col. ill. ; cm.
Includes index.
Summary : More than 100 easy recipes for North American bread machines.
ISBN 1-55209-493-6
1. Bread. 2. Automatic bread machines. I. Title
641.8/ 15 –dc21 2000   CIP

Published in Canada in 2000 by
Firefly Books Ltd.
3680 Victoria Park Avenue
Willowdale, Ontario
Canada M2H 3K1

Published in the United States in 2000 by
Firefly Books (U.S.) Inc.
P.O. Box 1338, Ellicott Station
Buffalo, New York
USA 14205

Produced by: Denise Schon Books Inc.
Design: Joanna Kubicki
Editor: Ruth Pincoe
Photography: Hal Roth
Food stylist: Shirley Ann Holmes
Prop stylist: Oksana Slavutych

Printed and bound in Canada by Friesens, Altona, Manitoba
Printed on acid-free paper

The Publisher acknowledges the financial support of the Government of Canada through the Book Publishing Industry Development Program for its publishing activities.

To my mother Margaret McFee for introducing me to home cooking and yeast baking when I was growing up.

To my husband Allan for his continued support, enthusiasm and love as well as his passion for good food and cooking.

acknowledgments

I would sincerely like to thank many individuals who made this book possible:

My colleague, mentor and friend, Margaret Howard, for recommending me to Denise Schon to write a book on bread machine baking, due to my experience.

My assistant and long time friend, Bev Watson, for her enthusiasm, encouragement, testing and feedback from her many book and bridge club tasters.

My husband, Allan, who had to live with a new high tech decor of breadmachines in almost every room of our house, but most of all for his enthusiasm when he walked in the door every night to new aromas and for his expert taste testing and assistance.

My colleague and friend, Sue Bailey, for her encouragement and assistance in preparing some breads for photography.

My food associates and the representatives from Robin Hood Multifoods Inc., Rogers Flour Company and Fleischmann's Yeast who provided information on ingredients.

The many companies who provided the various models of bread-machines for the testing: Sunbeam Inc., West Bend of Canada, Sanyo, Black and Decker, Panasonic and Philips.

My friend Pat Molnar for volunteering to be a hand model in some of the photography.

My nephew, Ryan McFee, for his expertise that helped keep this book in synch on the computer.

My neighbors, friends and family who offered feedback as they sampled the breads, purchased flour in United States for testing and offered freezer storage; and particularly my next-door neighbor, Frances Hickey, for her encouragement, assistance in photocopying and proofreading.

To Kirsten Hanson of Denise Schon Books, Joanna Kubicki, Ruth Pincoe, Oksana Slavutych and Hal Roth for their special skills that helped turn my manuscript into this beautiful book.

contents

In spite of today's fast pace of life, more and more people are discovering the satisfaction of home-baked breads, and bread machines have made that possible. If you make your own bread, you can also make healthy choices by controlling the amounts of fat, salt or sugar, and incorporating more grains, fruits and vegetables. You can also create a whole array of artisan breads. With the delicious and exciting flavors in this collection of recipes, I also find it's easier to consume the daily 5 to 12 servings of grain products that are recommended in the food guides. Bread is actually good for us! Some people have told me that they don't want a bread machine because they would end up eating too much bread. My answer is that the problem is not the bread but what you put on it. If you eat wonderful fresh bread that has fantastic flavor and an interesting texture, you don't need anything on it. If you want a topping you can choose low-fat vegetable or fruit spreads. Of course I haven't even mentioned the money you can save, or the tantalizing aromas of baking bread that welcome family, friends and B&B guests to your home or cottage.

For me, food and travel are inseparable. Whether it is a ski weekend in Ontario or a trip to the Mediterranean, I always find inspirations for recipe development. In the recipe introductions you will see a number of references to getaways or trips that have inspired some of the flavors. As I baked these breads in my kitchen, I truly enjoyed the blending of wonderful aromas, the delicious tastes and the memories of past culinary experiences.

I suggest that you start by reading the tips at the beginning of the book and then make one of the white or whole-grain breads from chapters 1 or 2. Whether you are looking for an interesting bread to toast at breakfast or a flavorful bread for sandwiches, I am sure you will find many recipes that appeal to you.

As a second step, move on to the more creative and exciting savory and sweet flavors in chapters 3 and 4. Some of the ingredients in these recipes may be little known in your region but in another part of the country they may be quite common. I truly enjoy exploring the world of different flavors and I find these "new" ingredients can add a whole new flavor dimension to an otherwise common bread. Be sure to ask your supermarket or specialty store manager about these ingredients; quite often they are willing to order special items for you.

You might also pick up an extra package of the ingredient or spice as a thoughtful gift for a bread-making friend. The more you bake, the more comfortable you will feel about making substitutions for ingredients you don't have on hand or that your family does not like.

The recipes in chapters 5, 6 and 7 will lure you to use the dough cycle of your machine for creative baking options. This irresistible collection of recipes will take you from dinner rolls, pizzas and artisan breads to coffeecakes and international favorites. As you try some of these unfamiliar shapes you will gain more confidence. In fact my good friend and assistant Bev Watson was hesitant about making many of these artisan breads but she was thrilled with the amazing results and the rave reviews she received from family, friends and tasters.

New bakers will appreciate More Hints in chapter 8. This chapter contains a collection of tips and ingredient information for continued successful results. So now, load the machine, push the button and enjoy these taste experiences.

Savory Cranberry and Nut Bread, page 54

Storing Your Bread Machine

Since counter space is usually at a premium, a new appliance is often relegated to a low cupboard. It is not easily accessible and therefore not used very much. I suggest you do as I have done: keep your bread machine on the floor in a corner of the kitchen or a nearby family room or laundry room (make sure the room is not cold in winter). You can bring the bread pan to the kitchen counter to fill or to remove the bread. If you do keep your machine on the counter, be sure to place it well back; during kneading some machines can "walk" off the edge. It happened to us once! If you keep your machine on the floor, you won't need to worry about that possibility.

Choosing Loaf Size

I recommend that you become familiar with your machine and try some of the manufacturer's recipes before you make any of the recipes in this book, since machines differ and some have unique features. You should also check the manual for the volume of the bread pan and the recommended number of cups of flour for your machine, before you decide on the size of loaf to make. If this information is not in your manual, you can measure the volume of the bread pan by filling it with water from a liquid measuring cup. Check the recipes to see the largest quantity of flour used, and remember that white-flour recipes will give largest volume.

For the recipes in this book, I have developed two sizes of bread-machine loaves: large and extra large. The large loaf (approximately 1 1/2 lb) can be made in machines with volume of at least 10 to 11 cups. The extra-large loaf (approximately 2 to 2 1/2 lb) can be made in machines with a volume of 12 to 15 cups.

It is not always possible to judge the volume of a bread machine from the loaf weight of the model. For example, 2-lb models vary a great deal in the volume of the bread pan and the space for rising between the top of pan and the lid. There are also extra-large 2-lb models as well as an increasing number of 2 1/2-lb horizontal or vertical machines on the market that are designed to handle the biggest extra-large loaves. The highest loaves are usually those made with only white flour or those that contain either egg or fruit or vegetable purée. Loaves made with whole wheat, grains or heavy ingredients do not rise as high. I recommend that you make a large loaf first (that is, the smaller of the two sizes, given in these recipes) with your choice of flour and yeast and see how it fits in your machine.

Assembling and Measuring Ingredients

If possible, arrange a central place in your cupboards for the dry ingredients (other than yeast) and measuring utensils so that you can load the machine quickly and efficiently.

I also keep salt and sugar in small jars or sealed containers for ease of measuring.

I suggest you assemble all the ingredients for a recipe on the counter or on a tray and put each container aside (or away) after you have added the ingredient to the pan. I also like to check off the ingredients on the recipe with a pencil. If an interruption such as the telephone causes you to forget an ingredient, the loaf might be ruined. You can also set ingredients that are to be added later (at the ingredient signal or raisin/nut beep) beside the machine as a reminder.

Accurate measurement of ingredients is crucial for success with a bread machine. I've tested all the recipes with the more common imperial measures, not metric measures. There is no easy and accurate conversion to metric in baking so I suggest you use imperial measuring cups and spoons when baking from this book.

There is an important difference between measuring utensils for dry ingredients and those for wet ingredients. Dry measures are usually sets of four nesting plastic or metal cups (1/4, 1/3, 1/2 and 1 cup). Liquid measures are usually made of transparent glass or plastic and come in 1-, 2- and 4-cup measures. Measuring spoons are used for both wet and dry ingredients and usually come in sets of four (1/4, 1/2 and 1 tsp as well as 1 tbsp). Some sets also have 1/2 tbsp, which is useful. I find it is handy, although not necessary, to have two sets of measuring spoons available, in case one is wet when you need to measure a dry ingredient. *Never measure ingredients over the pan.*

For Dry Ingredients: Spoon ingredients such as flour into the measuring cup and level it off with the straight edge of a knife. Don't scoop the flour with a measuring cup as this packs in extra flour and would result in heavy-textured bread. The one exception to this rule is brown sugar, which should

be packed into the measuring cup. *Never use liquid measures for dry ingredients.*

For Liquid Ingredients: Place the measuring cup on a level surface and pour in the liquid to the correct level; bend down to check the accuracy of your measurement at eye level. *Never use dry measures for liquids.*

For Fats: Measure soft butter and margarine by packing them into measuring spoons or dry measures and leveling off the top with the straight edge of a knife. Measure oils by pouring them into measuring spoons or liquid measures.

The Order of Ingredients and the Ingredient Signal

The ingredients for the recipes in this book are listed in the order recommended by many bread-machine manufacturers. However, you should follow the order of ingredients recommended in the manual for your machine. As a general rule, ingredients listed after the yeast are to be added later during the second

kneading cycle at an ingredient signal or raisin/nut beep. If your machine does not have this signal, check your manual to see when the second kneading starts and set a timer accordingly. If ingredients such as fruit or nuts are added too soon, they can be chopped too finely or puréed. See page 149 for tips about adding these ingredients.

Checking Doughs During Kneading

The recipes in this book have all been successfully tested in specific models of each of the brands of bread machines listed in the Acknowledgments. However, every brand and model has its own unique cycles and kneading patterns and these may change from year to year. I recommend that you do not adjust the quantities of ingredients for a recipe the first time you make it, unless the dough seems extremely wet or dry. If possible, make notes on the dough consistency at the ingredient signal or raisin/nut beep or during the second kneading. (Since some ingredients take longer to absorb moisture than others, you can't always judge during the first kneading.) For most of the recipes, you should end up with a smooth ball of dough. Some recipes produce a wetter, stickier dough and yet bake up perfectly — I've tried to indicate that in the Tips. If you hear the machine straining or stalling, add liquid, a tablespoon at a time, and double-check your measurements.

chapter one

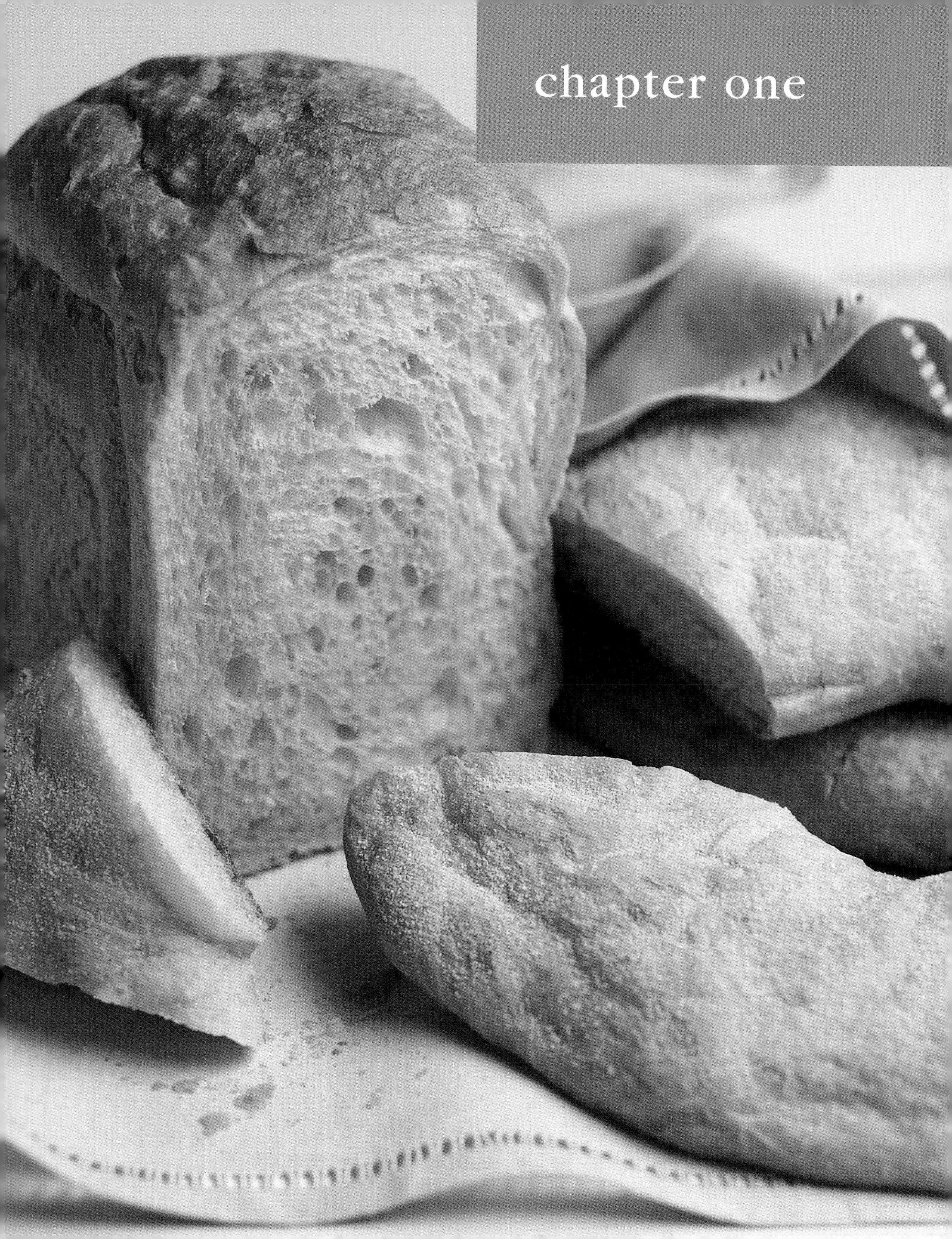

classic white bread

buttermilk bread

potato bread

french bread

crusty salt-free bread

quick 'n' easy mock sourdough

sourdough french bread

sourdough starter

gluten-free white bread

gluten-free triple corn bread

gluten-free cinnamon, fruit and
   raisin bread

This is a perfect place to start if you want white breads that most families will love. These breads bear little resemblance to packaged commercial varieties. Here you will find basic white breads — some fortified with or flavored with potato, yogurt, sourdough, cornmeal and buttermilk. The French and Sourdough recipes can also be made as doughs, shaped into loaves or buns and baked in a conventional oven if you choose. This chapter also includes several recipes for gluten-free breads with variations so that you can make tasty breads for family or friends who have an allergy to wheat.

classic white bread

The tender, close texture of this basic bread lends itself to endless variations. Change the flavor slightly by using olive oil or a flavored oil. Prepare the dough and choose one of the variations to make rolls, bread sticks or pretzels. The flowerpot loaves are perfect for an outdoor party or a unique gift.

LARGE	INGREDIENTS	EXTRA LARGE
1 1/4 cups	water	1 1/2 cups
1 tbsp	margarine, butter or vegetable oil	2 tbsp
3/4 tsp	salt	1 tsp
1 tbsp	sugar	2 tbsp
3 1/4 cups	white flour*	4 cups
2 tbsp	instant skim-milk powder	1/4 cup
1 1/4 tsp	bread-machine or instant yeast	1 1/2 tsp

*In Canada use all-purpose or bread flour; in the United States use bread flour.

1. Add all ingredients to machine according to manufacturer's directions. Select basic white bread cycle.

TIP
A good time saver is to create your own "bread mix" for your favorite recipe. You can package several batches at a time. Label zipper-style freezer bags with the recipe name and the amount of liquid and yeast to be added, then measure all the dry ingredients (except the yeast) into the bag. Store the bags in the refrigerator or freezer, and bring to room temperature before using. These custom bread mixes make a great gift for a hungry pizza-lover or a hostess with a bread machine and they can also entice children to use the bread machine.

VARIATIONS
Herb Bread
Add 2 to 3 tsp dried Italian seasoning or a purchased herb blend of your choice.

Rolls, Bread Sticks or Pretzels
Select dough cycle. When dough is finished, shape as desired for rolls (page 105), bread sticks (page 107), or pretzels (page 106).

Flowerpot Bread
Select dough cycle. Lightly grease clean small or medium 3- to 4-inch diameter clay flowerpots. When cycle is complete, remove dough to lightly floured surface; cover and let rest 5 to 10 minutes.
Cut dough into small balls that will fill flowerpots halfway. Cover and let rise in a warm place for 30 to 40 minutes or until almost doubled in size.
Bake at 375°F for 25 to 30 minutes, depending on size of pot, or until golden brown (or an instant-read thermometer inserted in center reads 200°F).

buttermilk bread

TIP

To toast sesame seeds place in non-stick skillet and cook over medium heat, shaking or stirring, until lightly browned. You can also purchase toasted sesame seeds in specialty stores.

VARIATION

Substitute fresh, warmed buttermilk for water. Omit buttermilk powder.

The word buttermilk signals high fat to some people but buttermilk is actually made from low-fat milk. It gives this bread a tangy tartness and a slightly yellow color, and the sesame seeds add texture. Look for buttermilk powder in bulk or health food stores. The powder keeps indefinitely.

LARGE	INGREDIENTS	EXTRA LARGE
1 1/4 cups	water	1 1/2 cups
2 tsp	vegetable oil, margarine or butter	1 tbsp
3/4 tsp	salt	1 tsp
2 tsp	sugar	1 tbsp
1/3 cup	buttermilk powder	1/2 cup
3 1/4 cups	white flour*	4 cups
3 tbsp	toasted or brown sesame seeds (optional)	1/4 cup
1 1/4 tsp	bread-machine or instant yeast	1 1/2 tsp

*In Canada use all-purpose or bread flour; in the United States use bread flour.

1. Add all ingredients to machine according to manufacturer's directions. Select basic white bread cycle.

potato bread

Pioneers used mashed potatoes to stretch the scarce, expensive wheat flour and to add moistness to their bread. Today we can use the convenience of instant mashed potato flakes to achieve the same moist, rich and compact results.

TIPS

Potatoes enhance the action of yeast so you may want to reduce the amount of yeast slightly.

Keep fresh garlic away from the yeast as it will inhibit the action of yeast.

VARIATIONS

Add 2 to 3 tsp dried chives or dill-weed.

Add 1 or 2 minced cloves of garlic and 2 to 3 tsp dried rosemary at the same time as the salt.

LARGE	INGREDIENTS	EXTRA LARGE
1 1/3 cups	water	1 2/3 cups
2 tbsp	vegetable oil, margarine or butter	3 tbsp
3/4 tsp	salt	1 tsp
1 tbsp	sugar	2 tbsp
2 tbsp	instant skim-milk powder	3 tbsp
3 1/4 cups	white flour*	4 cups
1/2 cup	instant mashed potato flakes	2/3 cup
1 tsp	bread-machine or instant yeast	1 1/4 tsp

*In Canada use all-purpose or bread flour; in the United States use bread flour.

1. Add all ingredients to machine according to manufacturer's directions. Select basic white bread cycle.

french bread

It is the lack of fat that gives French bread its extra-crispy crust. Baguettes were created in Paris to give customers more crisp crust on their bread. French bread comes in a variety of shapes and sizes, so why not try the oven-baked variations when you have time. You can also toast thick slices of baguette and top with chicken liver spread or tapenade, or rub the slices with garlic and top with an herbed tomato mixture to make bruschetta.

LARGE	INGREDIENTS	EXTRA LARGE
1 1/4 cups	water	1 1/2 cups
3/4 tsp	salt	1 tsp
1 tsp	sugar	1 1/2 tsp
3 1/4 cups	white flour*	4 cups
1 1/4 tsp	bread-machine or instant yeast	1 1/2 tsp

*In Canada use all-purpose flour or bread flour; in the United States use bread flour.

1. Add all ingredients to machine according to manufacturer's directions. Select French bread cycle.

Shaping and Baking Baguettes
Select dough cycle. When cycle is complete, remove dough to lightly floured surface; cover and let rest 5 to 10 minutes.

Divide dough into 2 pieces (large loaf) or 3 pieces (extra-large loaf). Roll each piece into a 14- or 15-inch rope. Place the ropes on cornmeal-coated baking sheets. Cover and let rise in warm place until doubled in size, about 45 to 60 minutes.

With a sharp knife make 3 diagonal slashes across the top of each baguette. Brush with cold water and place in cold oven. Place a shallow pan with about 1/2 inch of boiling water on the bottom shelf of oven. Set oven temperature at 425°F and bake for 20 to 30 minutes or until crust is golden brown and loaves sound hollow when tapped (or instant-read thermometer inserted in the center reads 200°F).

VARIATIONS
Bread sticks or Épi
Prepare dough as directed for baguettes and shape as desired for bread sticks (page 107) or for Épi (page 115).

Crusty Rolls
Yield: *12 or 16 rolls*
Prepare dough as directed for baguettes. Divide dough into 12 (large batch) or 16 (extra-large batch) pieces. Shape each piece into a smooth ball and place smooth side up on cornmeal-coated baking sheets. Cover and let rise about 30 to 40 minutes or until doubled in size.
Bake at 400°F for 20 to 25 minutes or until crusts are golden brown and buns sound hollow if tapped (or instant-read thermometer inserted in the center reads 200°F).

Pistolets
Yield: *12 or 16 rolls*
This shape is traditional to Belgium and Northern France. Shape dough into 12 (large batch) or 16 (extra-large batch) smooth balls and dust with flour. With handle of spoon make a deep indentation across the center of each ball, pressing down almost to the bottom. Sprinkle again with flour so the halves won't stick together during rising. Pull gently to lengthen roll and place on lightly greased baking sheet 2 inches apart. Cover, let rise and bake as directed for Crusty Rolls.

crusty salt-free bread

Years ago, salt was heavily taxed so the people of Tuscany often baked their bread without it. Today they enjoy salt-free bread with salty salami and cheeses. The beaten egg whites make the dough quite moist but they add extra crispiness to the crust — a good way to use up leftover egg whites from egg breads or custards.

LARGE	INGREDIENTS	EXTRA LARGE
1 cup	water	1 1/4 cups
1 tbsp	olive oil or vegetable oil	2 tbsp
1 1/2 tsp	sugar	1 tbsp
3 1/4 cups	white flour*	4 cups
1 1/4 tsp	bread-machine or instant yeast	1 1/2 tsp
2	large egg whites, stiffly beaten	3

*In Canada use all-purpose or bread flour; in the United States use bread flour.

1. Add all ingredients except egg whites to machine according to manufacturer's directions. Select French or basic white cycle.

2. Add egg whites after machine has started to mix and ingredients are moistened. If necessary, scrape down sides with rubber spatula once or twice.

quick 'n' easy mock sourdough

By adding yogurt and vinegar, you can give your bread a sourdough tang and avoid the extra step of making a sourdough starter. Alternatively, omit the vinegar and let your imagination guide your choice of fruit-flavored yogurts and juices. Use the oven-baked variation to create an artisan bread.

LARGE	INGREDIENTS	EXTRA LARGE
1 cup	low-fat yogurt	1 1/3 cup
1/3 cup	water	1/2 cup
2 tsp	vinegar	1 tbsp
3/4 tsp	salt	1 tsp
2 tsp	sugar	1 tbsp
3 cups	white flour*	4 cups
1 1/4 tsp	bread-machine or instant yeast	1 1/2 tsp

*In Canada use all-purpose or bread flour; in the United States use bread flour.

1. Add all ingredients to machine according to manufacturer's directions. Select French or basic white cycle.

TIPS
Drain off any accumulated liquid from top of yogurt.

If possible, check the dough consistency at the ingredient signal or 20 to 30 minutes into kneading cycle and adjust if necessary, since the consistency of yogurt can vary.

Although yogurt is not a dry ingredient, you may find it easier to measure in dry measuring cups.

VARIATIONS
Add 3 to 4 tbsp sesame seeds for a unique texture.

Substitute fruit-flavored yogurt for plain yogurt and substitute fruit juice for water.

Crusty Oven-baked Loaf
Select dough cycle. When complete remove dough to lightly floured surface. Cover and allow to rest 5 to 10 minutes.

For extra-large size, divide dough into 2 pieces; for large size, leave whole. Roll each piece of dough into a rectangle and then roll up jelly-roll style, sealing edges and ends. Place on lightly greased or parchment-lined baking sheet or perforated pizza pan. Cover and let rise in warm place for 30 to 40 minutes or until doubled in size.

Slash loaves diagonally 5 or 6 times with sharp knife and brush with cold water. Bake at 400°F for 20 to 25 minutes or until crust is golden brown and loaf sounds hollow if tapped (or an instant-read thermo-meter inserted in the center reads 200°F). For a crispier crust, brush or spray loaves with cold water 2 or 3 times during baking.

sourdough french bread

The starter is what gives sourdough bread its distinctive taste and texture. Flavors and results vary due to the variation in airborne yeast in different localities. Your bread may not have the flavor of San Francisco sourdough but it will still have a wonderful taste.

Since a sourdough starter gives an extra-large rise, I recommend making a large loaf unless you have an extra-large machine. If you have more time, try either size as an oven-baked loaf. The ring-shaped Couronne gives a higher proportion of crust to crumb and also makes a great layered sandwich loaf for a group. The Couronne was created in France for cyclists to put over their arm like a shopping basket.

LARGE	INGREDIENTS	EXTRA LARGE
1 1/2 cups	sourdough starter (page 22)	1 3/4 cups
1/2 cup	water	3/4 cup
3/4 tsp	salt	1 tsp
1 tbsp	sugar	2 tbsp
2 1/2 cups	white flour*	3 1/2 cups
1 tsp	bread-machine or instant yeast	1 tsp

*In Canada use all-purpose or bread flour; in the United States use bread flour.

1. Add all ingredients to machine according to manufacturer's directions. Select French or basic white bread cycle.

For a stronger sourdough flavor
Place the starter, water and 2/3 cup of flour in machine. Select dough cycle and allow to mix 5 minutes, scraping down sides with rubber spatula. Stop machine and leave mixture in machine for 24 to 36 hours. When ready to make bread, add remaining flour and ingredients. Select French or basic white cycle.

TIP
Commercial ovens have steam jets to keep bread moist during the initial rising in order to create a thin, crispy crust. To create a similar environment, brush the bread or spray the oven walls with cold water 2 or 3 times during baking.

VARIATIONS
Couronne or Ring Loaf
Select dough cycle. When cycle is complete, remove dough to lightly floured surface; cover and allow to rest 5 to 10 minutes.

Shape into 1 ball (large) or 2 balls (extra large), flatten slightly and place on lightly greased or parchment-lined baking sheet. Make a hole in middle and with floured hands push the dough out to create a 6-inch hole. Cover and let rise in warm place for about 30 to 45 minutes or until doubled in size.

Brush loaf with cold water, sprinkle top with cornmeal or flour if desired, and place in cold oven. Place a shallow pan on bottom shelf of oven, fill it with about 1/2 inch of boiling water and close oven door to trap steam. Set oven at 425°F and bake for 30 to 35 minutes or until crust is browned and loaf sounds hollow if tapped (or an instant-read thermometer inserted in center reads 200°F).

Crusty Sourdough Rolls
Select dough cycle; shape dough and bake as directed for French Crusty Rolls (page 17).

sourdough starter

Before commercial yeast became available, people used natural or wild yeast starters to leaven their bread. Sourdough starters, which we still use today, can be replenished, and many were passed on from family to family for generations.

If you are making oven-baked breads, you can use a sourdough starter that has been fed or replenished (as directed in the tips) and kept alive for many weeks. However, if you are making bread in the bread machine, I recommend using a starter that is no more than two weeks old; older starters contain uncontrollable wild yeast and may give unpredictable results. Most starters need to sit for at least 24 hours, but the flavor and texture will improve as the starter ages and develops. If you don't want the bother of keeping a starter in the refrigerator and feeding it, make just enough to use each time.

LARGE BATCH	INGREDIENTS	EXTRA-LARGE BATCH
3/4 tsp	bread-machine or instant yeast	1 1/2 tsp
1 cup	lukewarm water (105° to 110°F)	2 cups
1 cup	all-purpose flour	2 cups
1 1/2 tsp	instant skim-milk powder	1 tbsp

1. In large glass bowl dissolve yeast in water. Beat in remaining ingredients until smooth and mixture is like pancake batter. Loosely cover with wax paper and let stand at room temperature (75° to 85°F) for 2 to 3 days, stirring once a day until the mixture is bubbling, fermented and has a sour smell.

2. The starter is now ready to use in recipes. Starter can be stored in the refrigerator in a covered plastic container. Bring it to room temperature before using or put all the ingredients in the bread pan and set the delay cycle to start in 1 to 2 hours.

gluten-free white bread

Brown-rice flour has more flavor and nutritional value than white-rice flour because it retains some of the hull and bran from the rice kernel. Potato starch, which is milled from the starch of potatoes, helps retain moisture and aids the yeast fermentation. Do not use potato flour. This bread makes a great grilled-cheese sandwich. Try the variations to add variety to your menus.

INGREDIENTS

1 2/3 cups	water
3	large eggs
3 tbsp	vegetable oil, melted butter or margarine
1 tsp	salt
2 tbsp	sugar
1/2 cup	instant skim-milk powder
1 1/4 cups	white-rice flour
1 cup	brown-rice flour
2/3 cup	tapioca starch or flour
1/3 cup	potato starch
1 tbsp	xanthan gum
2 tsp	pectin crystals
2 tsp	bread-machine yeast

TIPS

If you have a super-express cycle (1 to 1 1/4 hours), use it to experiment with these gluten-free recipes.

Gluten-free breads tend to dry out fast. Wrap them tightly and store them in the refrigerator or freezer.

Buy fresh gluten-free flours and store them airtight in the refrigerator or freezer as they can go rancid; bring flour to room temperature before using.

Don't try to double these recipes, as the dough will be too heavy to rise properly.

If you use instant yeast, add 1 tsp white or cider vinegar.

VARIATION
Gluten-free Herbed Cheese Bread
Add 1 1/2 cups shredded old Cheddar cheese, 1 tbsp dried onion flakes, 1 clove minced garlic and 2 tsp dried dillweed or Italian seasoning with the salt. If desired add 1/2 tsp celery seed or fennel seed.

1. Add first 3 ingredients to bread machine pan and beat with plastic whisk or fork to mix well. Add rest of ingredients in the order given above. Select rapid or basic white cycle (approximately 2 to 3 hours). **2.** During first kneading cycle, scrape down sides of pan with rubber spatula. When bread is baked, remove from pan and cool on rack.

About Gluten-free breads
The consistency of gluten-free doughs is like a quick-bread batter. The finished loaves also look like quick breads but have flat tops and a coarse texture.

Since these doughs have no gluten, other products such as xanthan gum are needed to give structure and to trap the carbon dioxide given off by the yeast. Pectin or gelatin also help the structure and can be interchanged in the recipes. Use 1 tsp plain gelatin or 2 tsp pectin crystals for about 3 cups flour.

For best results, be sure ingredients are at room temperature. Whisk the wet ingredients to incorporate some air; stir the dry ingredients before measuring to incorporate air and lighten them a little.

Tapioca flour is processed from roots of the cassava plant.

gluten-free triple corn bread

TIPS
If you use instant yeast, add 1 tsp white or cider vinegar. Try this recipe on a super-express cycle (1 to 1 1/4 hours). Do not substitute potato flour for potato starch.

VARIATION
Gluten-free Mexican Corn Bread
Add 3/4 tsp each of dried thyme and oregano and 1/4 to 1/2 tsp dried chili peppers with the salt. (If desired, substitute 1 to 2 tsp hot green pepper sauce or 2 to 3 tbsp diced jalapeño peppers for the dried chili peppers.)

Cream-style corn, cornmeal and corn flour give extra flavor and texture to this moist bread. The addition of bean flour (made from whole dried white-pea, garbanzo, Romano or soy beans) provides protein and nutrients. Toast or grill slices of this corn bread and top with salsa or tomatoes and cheese for snacks or appetizers.

INGREDIENTS

1 cup	water
1 1/2 cups	cream-style corn
2 tbsp	vegetable oil, melted margarine or butter
3	large eggs
2 tbsp	honey
1 tsp	salt
1 cup	corn flour
1/2 cup	whole-bean flour
3/4 cup	cornstarch
1/2 cup	potato starch
1/4 cup	cornmeal
1/4 cup	tapioca starch
1 tbsp	xanthan gum
1 tsp	plain gelatin
2 tsp	bread-machine yeast

1. Add first 5 ingredients to bread machine pan and beat with plastic whisk or fork to mix. Add remaining ingredients in the order given above. Select rapid or basic white cycle (approximately 2 to 3 hours).

2. During the first kneading cycle, scrape down sides of pan with a rubber spatula. When bread is baked, remove from pan and cool on rack.

gluten-free cinnamon, fruit and raisin bread

Very ripe bananas or sweetened applesauce give the best flavor and make a moist bread to serve as a snack with tea or for dessert. This bread is also great toasted for breakfast.

TIPS
Replace 1/4 cup raisins with 1/4 cup chopped nuts.
If you use instant yeast, add 1 tsp white or cider vinegar.
Try this recipe on a super-express cycle (1 to 1 1/4 hours).
Do not substitute potato flour for potato starch.

INGREDIENTS

1 1/3 cups	water
3	large eggs
3 tbsp	vegetable oil, melted margarine or butter
2/3 cup	mashed ripe banana or applesauce
1 tsp	salt
3 tbsp	brown sugar
2 tbsp	instant skim-milk powder
2 cups	white-rice flour
2/3 cup	potato starch
1/3 cup	tapioca starch
1 tbsp	xanthan gum
1 tsp	plain gelatin
1 tbsp	ground cinnamon
2 tsp	bread-machine yeast
3/4 cup	raisins

1. Add first 4 ingredients to bread machine pan and beat with plastic whisk or fork to mix well. Add rest of ingredients in the order given above. Select rapid or basic white cycle (approximately 2 to 3 hours).

2. After 5 minutes of mixing, scrape down sides of pan with a rubber spatula. When bread is baked, remove from pan and cool on rack.

chapter two

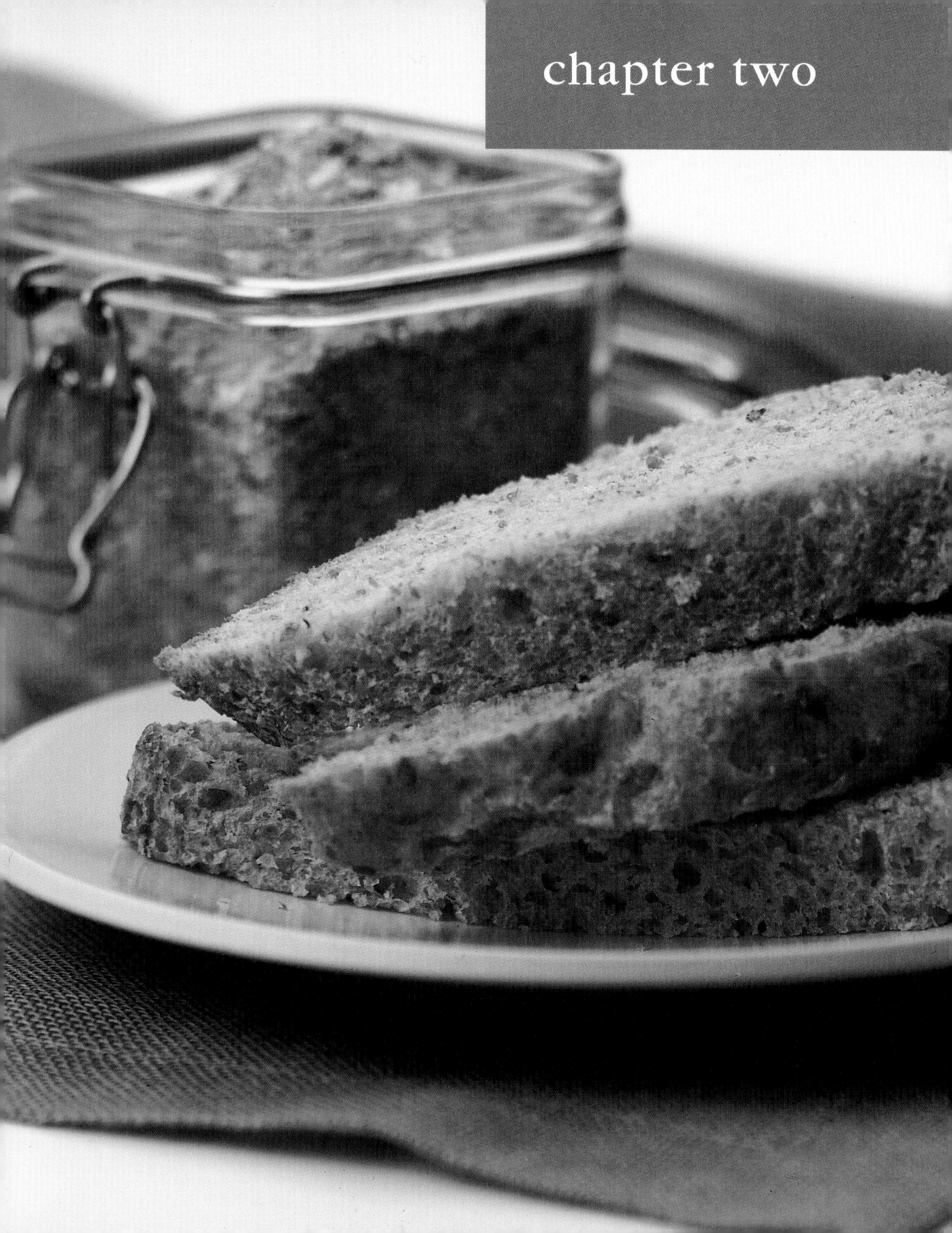

whole wheat, multigrain and other hearty breads

100% whole-wheat bread

light wheat and cornmeal bread

crunchy cracked-wheat bread

honey 'n' wheat
english-muffin bread

wholesome multigrain bread

walnut wheat berry bread

rustic grain bread

hovis bread

light rye bread

good hearth bread

spelt bread

Whole-grain ingredients add more nutrients and fiber and they produce breads with a dense, chewy texture and a fabulous taste. You may find, as I have, that you can win over some of those "white bread only eaters" with these recipes.

This chapter includes a basic 100% whole-wheat bread that is sweet and wholesome, and a 50% whole-wheat bread with cornmeal that has a honeycomb texture. There are also nutty multigrain breads, an English-muffin loaf, and a light rye. (For a darker rye, try the Deli Rye made with sauerkraut in chapter 3 or the oven-baked European Pumpernickel Bread in chapter 7.) Other recipes contain more unusual ingredients such as spelt, cracked wheat, bran, wheat berries and soy flour for the more adventurous baker.

100% whole-wheat bread

VARIATIONS
For a breakfast bread, add 1 1/2 to 2 tbsp grated orange rind to create a wonderful flavor complement to fruit jams.
For a crunchy texture substitute 1/2 cup multigrain cereal mix for 1/2 cup flour.

The egg gives this whole-wheat bread a light texture — great for toast and jam for breakfast or for sandwiches. For a milder flavor, use honey rather than molasses.

LARGE	INGREDIENTS	EXTRA LARGE
1 cup	water	1 1/3 cups
2 tbsp	vegetable oil, margarine or butter	3 tbsp
1	large egg	1
3/4 tsp	salt	1 tsp
2 tbsp	honey or molasses	3 tbsp
3 cups	whole-wheat flour	4 cups
1 1/4 tsp	bread-machine or instant yeast	1 1/4 tsp

1. Add all ingredients to machine according to manufacturer's directions. Select whole-wheat cycle (if available) or basic white cycle.

light wheat and cornmeal bread

This combination of whole-wheat flour and cornmeal was popular with all the tasters. The cornmeal gives this bread a nutty texture, a warm golden color and a honeycomb texture. However, you can substitute whole-wheat flour for the cornmeal if desired. Use leftovers to make croutons for soups or salads.

TIP
To make croutons, cut thick slices of leftover bread and brush both sides with oil. Cut slices into cubes and place in a single layer on an ungreased baking sheet. Bake at 325°F until crisp and golden, stirring occasionally.

VARIATION
Substitute whole-wheat flour for the cornmeal.

LARGE	INGREDIENTS	EXTRA LARGE
1 1/4 cups	water	1 1/2 cups
1 tbsp	vegetable oil, margarine or butter	2 tbsp
3/4 tsp	salt	1 tsp
3 tbsp	brown sugar, packed	1/4 cup
1 1/2 cups	white flour*	2 cups
1 cup	whole-wheat flour	1 1/3 cups
1/2 cup	cornmeal	3/4 cup
1 1/4 tsp	bread-machine or instant yeast	1 1/2 tsp

*In Canada use all-purpose or bread flour; in the United States use bread flour.

1. Add all ingredients to machine according to manufacturer's directions. Select whole-wheat cycle (if available) or basic white cycle.

crunchy cracked-wheat bread

Cracked wheat is made by breaking whole-wheat kernels into pieces; it is used to add texture and fiber to bread. Cracked wheat is often soaked or pre-cooked, but, like many of my testers, I prefer to leave it raw for a crunchier texture. For a change of flavor, use the buttermilk variation. This hearty bread is great for toast or served with soup.

LARGE	INGREDIENTS	EXTRA LARGE
1 1/4 cups	water	1 1/2 cups
2 tbsp	vegetable oil, margarine or butter	3 tbsp
2 tbsp	brown sugar, packed	3 tbsp
3/4 tsp	salt	1 tsp
3 tbsp	instant skim-milk powder	1/4 cup
1 1/2 cups	white flour*	2 cups
1 1/2 cups	whole-wheat flour	1 3/4 cups
3/4 cup	cracked wheat	1 cup
1 1/4 tsp	bread-machine or instant yeast	1 1/2 tsp

*In Canada use all-purpose or bread flour; in the United States use bread flour.

1. Add all ingredients to machine according to manufacturer's directions. Select whole-wheat cycle (if available) or basic white cycle.

honey 'n' wheat english-muffin bread

This is a great no-fat bread to bake overnight on the delay-start timer for breakfast. Don't be alarmed if you get a sunken top — it occurs naturally with the traditional coarse texture.

TIP
Try spraying the interior of the pan with cooking spray or oil if you have trouble getting this fat-free bread out of the pan.

VARIATION
Cinnamon-raisin Bread
Substitute white flour for whole-wheat flour (if desired), add 1 1/2 to 2 tsp ground cinnamon and use the raisins.

LARGE	INGREDIENTS	EXTRA LARGE
1 1/3 cups	water	1 2/3 cups
1 tbsp	honey	1 1/2 tbsp
3/4 tsp	salt	1 tsp
1/8 tsp	baking soda	1/4 tsp
3 tbsp	instant skim-milk powder	1/4 cup
2 cups	white flour*	2 1/2 cups
1 cup	whole-wheat flour	1 1/2 cups
1 1/4 tsp	bread-machine or instant yeast	1 1/4 tsp
1/2 cup	raisins (optional)	3/4 cup

*In Canada use all-purpose or bread flour; in the United States use bread flour.

1. Add all ingredients except raisins to machine according to manufacturer's directions. Select basic white or whole-wheat cycle.

2. Add raisins at ingredient signal (about 20 to 30 minutes into cycle).

wholesome multigrain bread

Everyone's favorite — a high-fiber, crunchy-textured bread. My good friend Elaine Duffy calls this "bird-seed bread." We enjoy it for breakfast instead of porridge. This recipe uses a multigrain cereal, which is more convenient than measuring a number of individual grains. If you prefer a less crunchy texture, try the Porridge Bread variation.

LARGE	INGREDIENTS	EXTRA LARGE
1 1/4 cups	water	1 1/2 cups
2 tbsp	vegetable oil, margarine or butter	3 tbsp
3/4 tsp	salt	1 tsp
3 tbsp	brown sugar, packed	1/4 cup
1 1/2 cups	white flour*	2 cups
1 cup	whole-wheat flour	1 cup
1/3 cup	oat bran	1/2 cup
2/3 cup	multigrain cereal mix (5 to 12 grain)	1 cup
1 1/4 tsp	bread-machine or instant yeast	1 1/2 tsp

*In Canada use all-purpose or bread flour; in the United States use bread flour.

1. Add all ingredients to machine according to manufacturer's directions. Select whole-wheat cycle (if available) or basic white cycle.

TIP

Cereal mixes usually contain a number of grains and seeds (such as cracked wheat, barley, durum wheat, rye or soy grits, cornmeal, millet, cracked triticale, rolled oats, and sunflower seeds, sesame seeds or flaxseed). You can find a variety of cereal mixes in health food stores or bulk sections of supermarkets, and some commercial mixtures, such as Red River, Brex or Sunny Boy, are more widely available.

VARIATION
Porridge Bread
Yield: *1 large loaf*
In medium saucepan combine 1/2 cup multigrain cereal mix with 1 1/4 cups hot water; bring to boil and cook 5 minutes. Cool to room temperature. Add porridge, 1/2 cup water, 2 tbsp vegetable oil, margarine or butter, 3/4 tsp salt, 3 tbsp honey, 3 cups white flour and 1 1/4 tsp bread-machine or instant yeast to machine according to manufacturer's directions. Select whole-wheat cycle (if available) or basic white cycle.

walnut wheat berry bread

One cold wintry day, my good friend and home economist Elaine Duffy served me a version of this bread that she was testing for her cooking school, along with a bowl of black bean soup. Since then it has been one of my favorites. It is also wonderful with cheese and fruit or cut into small finger shapes and served with Cheddar, brie or stilton cheese and a glass of sherry.

LARGE	INGREDIENTS	EXTRA LARGE
1/3 cup	wheat berries, soaked (see Tips)	1/2 cup
1 1/4 cups	water	1 1/2 cups
1 tbsp	vegetable oil, margarine or butter	2 tbsp
3/4 tsp	salt	1 tsp
2 tbsp	honey or maple syrup	3 tbsp
1 1/2 cups	white flour*	2 cups
1 1/2 cups	whole-wheat flour	2 cups
2 tbsp	wheat germ (optional)	3 tbsp
1 1/4 tsp	bread-machine or instant yeast	1 1/4 tsp
3/4 cup	coarsely chopped California walnuts	1 cup

*In Canada use all-purpose or bread flour; in the United States use bread flour.

1. Add all ingredients except nuts to machine according to manufacturer's directions. Select whole-wheat cycle (if available) or basic white cycle.

2. Add nuts at ingredient signal (or about 20 to 30 minutes into cycle).

TIPS

Wheat berries (or whole-wheat kernels) are usually soaked or cooked before adding to the dough and they give a chewy texture to the bread.

To soak wheat berries, place in small saucepan, cover generously with water, bring to boil and cook 15 minutes. Turn off heat and let stand overnight or at least 8 hours. Drain off excess liquid and use as directed in recipe.

Wheat germ, the embryo of the wheat kernel, adds nutrients and a nutty flavor to breads. Look for wheat germ in the cereal section of supermarkets or health food stores. Wheat germ contains oils that can go rancid so it should be refrigerated. If frozen the vitamin E can be destroyed.

California walnuts are sweeter and less bitter than other varieties of walnuts. To intensify the walnut flavor, use walnut oil instead of butter or margarine, and toast the walnuts.

VARIATION

Omit the nuts if desired. The wheat berries will still give the bread a crunchy texture.

rustic grain bread

TIP

Barley flakes are made from unbulled grain and have a pale gray color. Until two centuries ago, barley was the main grain used for bread in continental Europe. It adds a mild nutty flavor. Today, barley is more commonly known and available in the processed form of pearl barley (steamed, polished grains of barley with the bulls removed). Pearl barley is usually used to thicken soups, but should not be used in this recipe.

The grains in this recipe — rolled oats, rye flakes and barley flakes — are toasted to intensify the flavor (see Toasted Grain Mix, below). Rolled oats are familiar and readily available, and you can usually find rye flakes and barley flakes in health food stores. Rye flakes are made by heating whole grains of rye and pressing them, in a process similar to that for making rolled oats. Both rye and barley have very little gluten and so need to be combined with wheat flour in bread recipes.

LARGE	INGREDIENTS	EXTRA LARGE
1 1/4 cups	water	1 1/2 cups
2 tbsp	vegetable oil, margarine or butter	3 tbsp
3/4 tsp	salt	1 tsp
2 tbsp	liquid honey or molasses	3 tbsp
2 1/2 cups	white flour*	3 cups
1/2 cup	Toasted Grain Mix (see below)	3/4 cup
1/4 cup	cracked wheat	1/3 cup
1 1/4 tsp	bread-machine or instant yeast	1 1/2 tsp

*In Canada use all-purpose or bread flour; in the United States use bread flour.

1. Add all ingredients to machine according to manufacturer's directions. Select basic white or whole-wheat cycle.

Toasted Grain Mix
Combine 1 cup each of barley flakes, rye flakes and rolled oats on a shallow baking sheet. Toast in a 350°F oven for 30 minutes, stirring once. Set aside to cool. Toasted grains keep well in a sealed plastic container or bag in refrigerator or freezer.

If desired, double the quantity so you will have a good supply on hand for this recipe.

hovis bread

In the early stages of researching for this book, my assistant Bev Watson said that some of her tasters had requested a recipe for Hovis bread. Hovis flour was developed in England in the 1880s by Richard Smith. Made by adding a concentrated form of wheat germ to white flour, it became known as "Smith's Patent Germ Flour." The company that marketed the flour organized a national competition to find a new name for the increasingly popular bread and the word "Hovis" won. A London student constructed it from the Latin phrase *hominis vis*, the strength of man. It is a dense, substantial loaf with a rough-textured top and mild nutty flavor.

LARGE	INGREDIENTS	EXTRA LARGE
1 1/4 cups	water	1 1/2 cups
1 tbsp	vegetable oil, margarine or butter	2 tbsp
1 tbsp	vinegar	5 tsp
3/4 tsp	salt	1 tsp
2 tbsp	brown sugar, packed	3 tbsp
1 1/2 cups	white flour*	2 cups
1 cup	whole-wheat flour	1 1/2 cups
1/2 cup	soy flour	2/3 cup
1/3 cup	wheat germ	1/2 cup
1 1/4 tsp	bread-machine or instant yeast	1 1/2 tsp

*In Canada use all-purpose flour or bread flour; in the United States use bread flour.

VARIATION
You can substitute rice flour for soy flour if desired, although it is not as nutritious.

1. Add all ingredients to machine according to manufacturer's directions. Select whole-wheat cycle (if available) or basic white cycle.

east coast brown bread

This interesting variation of a Maritime specialty that was often served with baked beans comes from my friend Trudy Adsett and her East Coast relatives. It has a heavier texture than some breads and has become a favorite served with bean soups or stews, topped with tangy old Cheddar cheese or toasted for breakfast.

TIP
Substitute crumbled spoon-size shredded-wheat breakfast cereal for the crumbled shredded-wheat biscuits; use 1/3 cup for a large loaf or 1/2 cup for an extra-large loaf.

LARGE	INGREDIENTS	EXTRA LARGE
1 1/4 cups	water	1 1/2 cups
1 tbsp	vegetable oil, margarine or butter	2 tbsp
2 tbsp	molasses	3 tbsp
3/4 tsp	salt	1 tsp
2 tbsp	brown sugar, packed	3 tbsp
3 tbsp	instant skim-milk powder	1/4 cup
3 cups	white flour*	4 cups
1/2 cup	crumbled shredded-wheat biscuit	3/4 cup
1/2 cup	Grape-nuts™ (wheat and barley nuggets breakfast cereal)	3/4 cup
1 1/4 tsp	bread-machine or instant yeast	1 1/2 tsp

*In Canada use all-purpose or bread flour; in the United States use bread flour.

1. Add all ingredients to machine according to manufacturer's directions. Select basic white or whole-wheat cycle.

light rye bread

Rye is a hardy grain that grows well in wet climates. Several types of rye flour, including dark, medium and light, are available today; you can use any type, but I recommend the medium or the dark. Since rye flour is low in gluten, it is best combined with wheat flour. The molasses in this recipe gives the bread a darker color and a richer flavor that is wonderful for corned-beef sandwiches. Try the beer variation for a change in flavor. For a darker rye try the European Pumpernickel Bread in chapter 7 (page 131); for a savory dense loaf try Deli Rye in chapter 3 (page 56).

TIPS

Rye flour must be fresh for successful bread-machine loaves. If your flour is not fresh, try adding gluten flour as suggested for U.S. flours.

Stone-ground rye flour may result in a heavier, lower-volume loaf.

VARIATIONS

Use both caraway and dill seeds for a different flavor.

Substitute flat, room-temperature beer for the water; dark beers will add more flavor.

LARGE	INGREDIENTS	EXTRA LARGE
1 cup	water	1 1/4 cups
2 tbsp	vegetable oil, margarine or butter	3 tbsp
3/4 tsp	salt	1 tsp
2 tbsp	molasses or honey	3 tbsp
2 cups	white flour*	2 3/4 cups
1 cup	rye flour**	1 1/4 cups
2 tsp	caraway or dill seeds (optional)	1 tbsp
1 1/4 tsp	bread-machine or instant yeast	1 1/2 tsp

*In Canada use all-purpose flour or bread flour; in the United States use bread flour.
**In the United States add 2 tbsp gluten flour for a large loaf or 3 tbsp for an extra-large loaf. (See Gluten on page 147.) In Canada, you may wish to substitute a specialty blend of rye flour and enriched wheat flour for the white and rye flours. Reduce yeast by 1/2 tsp, if desired, for a denser texture.

1. Add all ingredients to machine according to manufacturer's directions. Select basic white, whole-wheat or rye cycle.

good hearth bread

Buckwheat is rich in B vitamins and it adds a distinctive tart taste and texture to this hearty bread. The flaxseed and mustard seeds add both texture and fiber, and flax also contains important essential nutrients. Buckwheat groats are usually pre-soaked, but in this recipe they are simply added to the bread pan with the water. Serve this tasty bread toasted with honey for breakfast.

LARGE	INGREDIENTS	EXTRA LARGE
1 1/4 cups	water	1 2/3 cups
1/3 cup	buckwheat groats	1/2 cup
2 tbsp	vegetable oil, margarine or butter	3 tbsp
3/4 tsp	salt	1 tsp
2 tbsp	brown sugar, packed	3 tbsp
1 1/2 cups	white flour*	2 cups
3/4 cup	whole-wheat flour	1 cup
1/2 cup	rye flour	3/4 cup
2 tbsp	each flaxseed and mustard seeds	3 tbsp
1 1/4 tsp	bread-machine or instant yeast	1 1/2 tsp

*In Canada use all-purpose or bread flour; in the United States use bread flour.

1. Add all ingredients to machine according to manufacturer's directions. Select basic white or whole-wheat cycle.

spelt bread

Spelt is a grain that is low in gluten but high in protein. It can be substituted for whole-wheat flour and can be tolerated by some people who are allergic to wheat. Used here without other flours it produces a heavy, dense-textured bread. My neighbor Norah Chaloner says that its firm texture makes it a good base for toasted open-face sandwiches. The fennel or anise seed adds a subtle flavor to the nuttiness of the spelt.

TIP

For a lighter-textured spelt bread try the Ancient Grain, Seed and Fruit Loaf on page 80.

LARGE	INGREDIENTS	EXTRA LARGE
1 cup	water	1 1/3 cups
2 tbsp	vegetable oil, margarine or butter	3 tbsp
1	large egg	1
3/4 tsp	salt	1 tsp
3 tbsp	brown sugar, packed	1/4 cup
4 cups	whole-grain spelt flour	5 cups
2 tsp	fennel or anise seed (optional)	1 tbsp
1 1/4 tsp	bread-machine or instant yeast	1 1/2 tsp

1. Add all ingredients to machine according to manufacturer's directions. Select whole-wheat cycle (if available) or basic white cycle.

chapter three

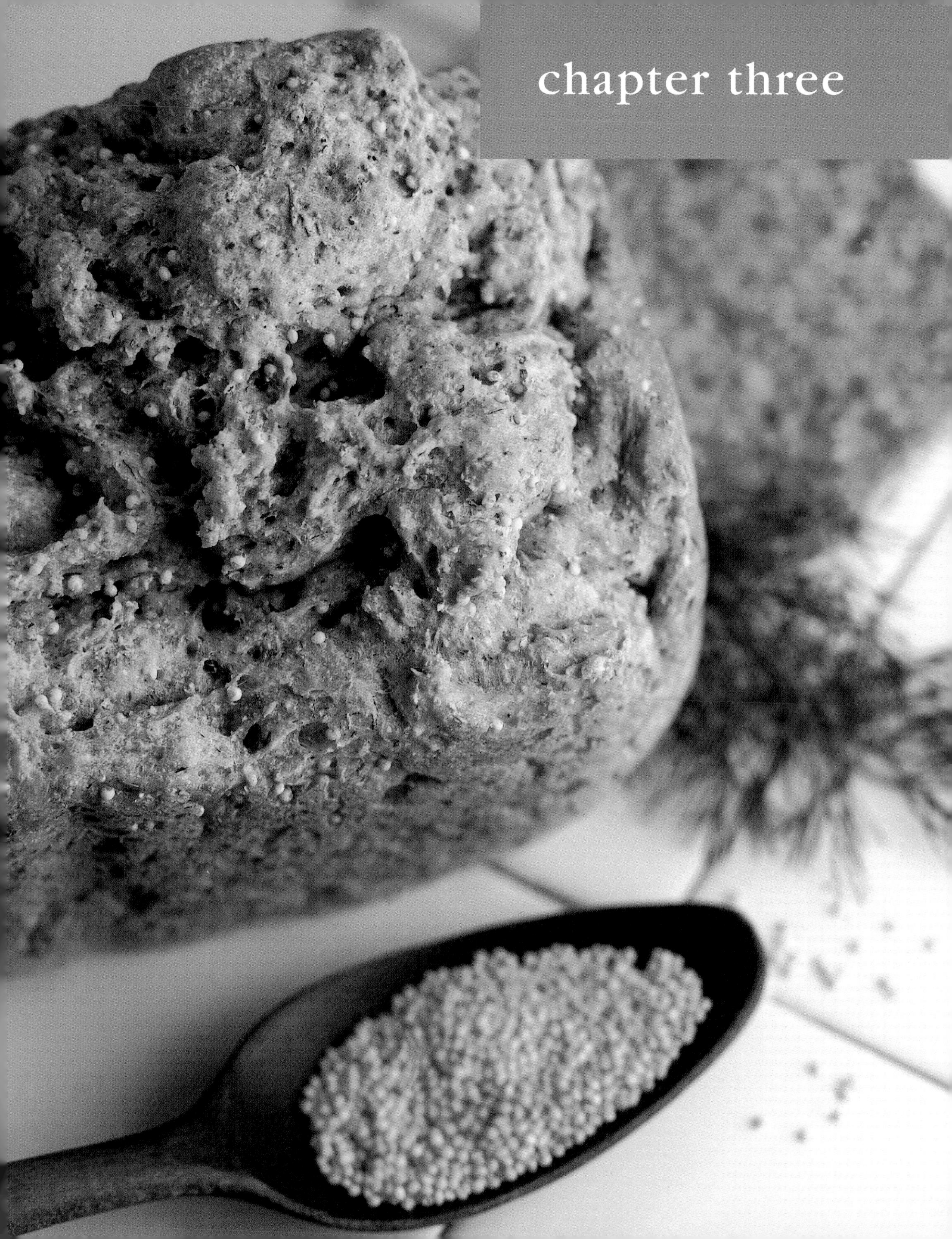

savory herb, seed and vegetable breads

This chapter includes full-flavored breads that go beyond the basic white and grainy brown breads in chapters 1 and 2.

Some are so nutrition-packed that they are almost a meal in themselves. Extra enriching ingredients include cheese (Cottage Cheese and Onion Bread, Confetti Cheese Bread), yogurt (Cajun Cornmeal Bread), seeds (Hearty Seed Bread), vegetables (Carrot Ginger Bread, Savory Sweet Potato Bread) and nuts (Savory Cranberry and Nut Bread). The Savory Sweet Potato Bread dough can also be shaped into dinner rolls and baked in the oven. All these breads make wonderful accompaniments to soups, salads or meals as well as tasty sandwiches. I hope that the interesting combinations will tempt you to make and enjoy the rich herbal flavors and bouquets.

cottage cheese and onion bread

cajun cornmeal bread

confetti cheese bread

hearty seed bread

pesto and sun-dried tomato bread

herbed millet bread

savory cranberry and nut bread

roasted red pepper and cheese bread

deli rye bread

roasted garlic bread

savory sweet potato bread

tomato-pepper bread

carrot ginger bread

cottage cheese and onion bread

VARIATIONS
Substitute dried chives for the parsley and omit onion flakes. Substitute 2 to 3 tsp dried dillweed for the parsley.

My assistant and friend Bev Watson made an enjoyable grilled cheese and tomato sandwich with this rich moist bread. It can also be used to add protein to vegetarian soup-and-sandwich meals.

LARGE	INGREDIENTS	EXTRA LARGE
1/2 cup	water	3/4 cup
1 cup	low-fat cottage cheese	1 1/2 cups
1	large egg	1
2 tbsp	vegetable oil, margarine or butter	3 tbsp
1/2 tsp	salt	3/4 tsp
2 tbsp	instant skim-milk powder	1/4 cup
3 1/4 cups	white flour*	4 cups
3 tbsp	dried parsley flakes (optional)	1/4 cup
1 1/2 tbsp	dried onion flakes	2 tbsp
1 1/4 tsp	bread-machine or instant yeast	1 1/4 tsp

*In Canada use all-purpose or bread flour; in the United States use bread flour.

1. Add all ingredients to machine according to manufacturer's directions. Select basic white bread cycle.

cajun cornmeal bread

Native peoples of North America used ground corn to make non-leavened breads. Since cornmeal has no gluten, it must be combined with wheat flour if it is used for yeast doughs. It gives an interesting texture and a slightly sweet flavor. Cornmeal is made from yellow, white or blue corn, but I recommend the yellow variety for this recipe. For appetizers or snacks, top toasted slices with salsa and Monterey Jack cheese. Leftovers make great croutons or stuffing.

TIPS
Drain liquid off yogurt before measuring. You may find it easier to measure yogurt in dry measures.
   Check the dough at the ingredient signal (or 20 to 30 minutes into the cycle) and adjust the consistency if necessary, since the consistency of yogurts and the moisture in peppers can vary.

LARGE	INGREDIENTS	EXTRA LARGE
1 cup	water	1 1/4 cups
1/2 cup	low-fat yogurt	3/4 cup
2 tbsp	olive oil or vegetable oil	3 tbsp
3/4 tsp	salt	1 tsp
2 tsp	sugar	1 tbsp
2 3/4 cup	white flour*	3 1/2 cups
3/4 cup	cornmeal	1 cup
1/2 tsp	oregano	3/4 tsp
1/4 tsp	each garlic powder, dried thyme and basil	1/2 tsp
1 1/4 tsp	bread-machine or instant yeast	1 1/2 tsp
3 tbsp	minced jalapeño pepper	1/4 cup
1/3 cup	diced sweet red pepper	1/2 cup

*In Canada use all-purpose or bread flour; in the United States use bread flour.

VARIATIONS
Substitute well-drained, canned jalapeño peppers for fresh. You could also use green hot pepper sauce to taste but remember to cut back the water by the same amount.
   Substitute green pepper for the red pepper, and 1/4 to 1/2 tsp chili powder for the minced jalapeño peppers.

1. Add all ingredients except peppers to machine according to manufacturer's directions. Select basic white cycle.
2. Add peppers at ingredient signal (or 20 to 30 minutes into the cycle).

A Gift from Your Kitchen
My friend Elaine Duffy, who runs a cooking school, came up with a novel gift idea for a bread-machine owner. Choose a clean, attractive, tall bottle or jar (such as a vinegar, oil or salad dressing bottle) that will just hold the dry ingredients required for this recipe.

   Combine the flour, salt and sugar. Using a funnel, fill the bottle on an angle with alternate layers of the flour mixture and cornmeal and finish with a layer of seasonings. Seal the yeast in plastic wrap and place it on top. Put the lid on the jar, attach a copy of the recipe with a ribbon and add other decoration as desired.

confetti cheese bread

The inspiration for this recipe came from a bread made by a local bakery a few years ago. The vegetables give the loaf a confetti-like appearance. The first time I served this bread to friends, it was gone in no time! A slice or two makes a complete lunch but it is also a wonderful accompaniment to soup or salads.

TIPS

The moisture content of the vegetables can vary. Check the dough when you add the cheese and adjust the consistency if necessary.

Put cheese in the freezer for 30 minutes before adding so it won't melt too quickly.

VARIATION

Substitute a mixture of dried basil, oregano and thyme for commercial Italian seasonings.

LARGE	INGREDIENTS	EXTRA LARGE
3/4 cup	water	1 cup
3/4 tsp	salt	1 tsp
1 tbsp	sugar	2 tbsp
2 tbsp	instant skim-milk powder	3 tbsp
1/2 cup	shredded carrot, lightly packed	2/3 cup
1/3 cup	each diced sweet green and red pepper	1/2 cup
3 cups	white flour*	4 cups
2 tsp	dried Italian seasoning	1 tbsp
1 1/4 tsp	bread-machine or instant yeast	1 1/4
3/4 cup	coarsely diced old Cheddar cheese	1 cup

*In Canada use all-purpose or bread flour; in the United States use bread flour.

1. Add all ingredients except cheese to machine according to manufacturer's directions. Select basic white cycle.
2. Add cheese at ingredient signal (or about 20 to 30 minutes into the cycle).

3. Remove loaf immediately after baking, since it is very tender.

hearty seed bread

This nutritious and robust loaf was inspired by a favorite bread served at a local restaurant. Vary the seeds as you wish. Aromatic cumin seeds look like caraway seeds but they have a very different and distinctive flavor that is good with Middle Eastern dishes or curries. Flaxseed provides contrasting color and texture and also adds essential nutrients and fiber.

LARGE	INGREDIENTS	EXTRA LARGE
1 1/3 cups	water	1 2/3 cups
1 tbsp	vegetable oil	2 tbsp
3/4 tsp	salt	1 tsp
2 tbsp	honey	3 tbsp
1 1/2 cups	white flour*	2 cups
1 1/2 cups	whole-wheat flour	2 cups
2 tbsp	each sesame seeds, unsalted sunflower seeds and poppy seeds	3 tbsp
3 tbsp	brown or golden flaxseed	1/4 cup
1 tsp	cumin seed (optional)	1 1/4 tsp
1 1/4 tsp	bread-machine or instant yeast	1 1/2 tsp

*In Canada use all-purpose or bread flour; in the United States use bread flour.

1. Add all ingredients to machine according to manufacturer's directions. Select whole-wheat cycle (if available) or basic white cycle.

pesto and sun-dried tomato bread

Pesto, the classic Italian sauce that originated in Genoa, is traditionally made with garlic, basil, pine nuts, olive oil and Parmesan cheese. You can either use commercial pesto or make your own. This bread adds a wonderful flavor to tomato, chicken or cream cheese sandwiches. It's also great for snacks or served with salads.

LARGE	INGREDIENTS	EXTRA LARGE
1 cup	water	1 1/4 cup
1/3 cup	pesto sauce	1/2 cup
3/4 tsp	salt	1 tsp
2 tsp	sugar	1 tbsp
1 tsp	minced garlic	1 1/2 tsp
3 cups	white flour*	4 cups
1/3 cup	chopped sun-dried tomatoes	1/2 cup
1/8 tsp	pepper or dried chili peppers (optional)	1/4 tsp
1 1/4 tsp	bread-machine or instant yeast	1 1/4 tsp

*In Canada use all-purpose or bread flour; in the United States use bread flour.

1. Add all ingredients to machine according to manufacturer's directions. Select basic white cycle.

TIPS

The consistency of commercial or homemade pesto sauce may vary. Check the dough at the ingredient signal (or about 20 to 30 minutes into the cycle) and adjust the consistency if necessary.

Sun-dried or oven-dried tomatoes that have not been packed in oil are best for this recipe and can be added with the other ingredients. If you use oil-packed ones, pat them dry and add at the ingredient signal (or 20 to 30 minutes into the cycle) or they will purée during the kneading.

Make pesto in the summer when basil is in abundance, freeze it in ice cube containers, then seal the pesto cubes in plastic bags so you can thaw small quantities as needed.

Be sure that fresh garlic does not touch the yeast as it will inhibit the rising action.

VARIATION

Experiment with other homemade pesto-type sauces made with cilantro, mint, dill, parsley or spinach. Omit the tomatoes if desired.

herbed millet bread

Millet is a tiny round grain that looks a lot like mustard seed and has a distinctly mild, sweet flavor. It gives this hearty bread a nutty texture and it also adds nutrients. This bread often has an interesting rough-textured top. Serve it with hearty soups or use it to add flavor to sandwiches.

TIP
Look for millet in health food or Asian food stores.

LARGE	INGREDIENTS	EXTRA LARGE
1 1/4 cups	water	1 1/2 cups
1 tbsp	vegetable oil, margarine or butter	2 tbsp
3/4 tsp	salt	1 tsp
2 tbsp	brown sugar, packed	3 tbsp
1 1/2 cups	white flour*	2 cups
1 1/2 cups	whole-wheat flour	2 cups
1/4 cup	millet	1/3 cup
3/4 tsp	dried dillweed	1 tsp
1/2 tsp	dried thyme	3/4 tsp
1 tbsp	each dried parsley and onion flakes	2 tbsp
1 1/4 tsp	bread-machine or instant yeast	1 1/2 tsp

*In Canada use all-purpose or bread flour; in the United States use bread flour.

1. Add all ingredients to machine according to manufacturer's directions. Select whole-wheat cycle (if available) or basic white cycle.

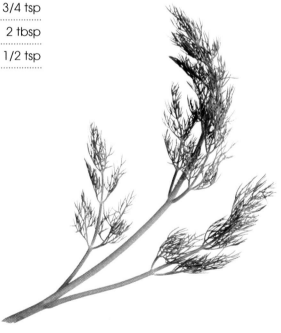

savory cranberry and nut bread

The concept for this recipe came from my daughter Cindy who enjoyed buns flavored with nuts and cranberries from a bakery in British Columbia at Thanksgiving. There is no sugar in this loaf; all the sweetness comes from the cranberries, and the seasonings are reminiscent of turkey stuffing. This deluxe bread is delicious on its own or spread with cream cheese for a snack, and it makes wonderful turkey sandwiches. In fact my friend and assistant Bev Watson said the loaf she was testing was so yummy she just had to go out and buy some turkey for a sandwich. If you are lucky enough to have any bread left over, it will make terrific stuffing for poultry or pork.

LARGE	INGREDIENTS	EXTRA LARGE
1 1/4 cups	water	1 1/2 cups
2 tbsp	vegetable oil, margarine or butter	3 tbsp
3/4 tsp	salt	1 tsp
3 cups	white flour*	4 cups
3 tbsp	dried onion flakes	1/4 cup
1 tsp	each dried rubbed sage leaves and savory leaves	1 1/2 tsp
1/8 tsp	pepper	1/4 tsp
1 1/4 tsp	bread-machine or instant yeast	1 1/4 tsp
2/3 cup	each dried cranberries and chopped pecans or walnuts	1 cup

*In Canada use all-purpose or bread flour; in the United States use bread flour.

1. Add all ingredients except cranberries and nuts to machine according to manufacturer's directions. Select basic white bread cycle.

2. Add fruit and nuts at ingredient signal (or 20 to 30 minutes into cycle).

roasted red pepper and cheese bread

I prefer creamy chèvre (goat cheese) for this bread because it gives a subtle tangy flavor and it is low in cholesterol and calories. However, if you don't like chèvre, try softened herb cream cheese. This is a wonderful bread to serve with salads or garlic soup. For an appetizer, top it with tapenade or olive paste. For a sandwich, fill it with grilled eggplant or zucchini.

TIPS

Roast, peel and freeze peppers when they are in abundance and less expensive.

For convenience buy peeled roasted peppers from the deli or in bottles.

Cut peppers in large pieces; you may get pretty red flecks throughout the bread, depending on the kneading action of your machine.

Do not substitute pimento (pickled peppers) for the peeled roasted peppers.

LARGE	INGREDIENTS	EXTRA LARGE
1/2 cup	water	3/4 cup
1	large egg	1 plus 1 yolk
2 tbsp	olive or vegetable oil	3 tbsp
3 oz (about 1/3 cup)	creamy goat cheese or softened herb cream cheese	4 oz (about 1/2 cup)
1/4 cup	roasted peeled red pepper pieces	1/3 cup
3/4 tsp	salt	1 tsp
2 tsp	sugar	1 tbsp
2 tbsp	instant skim-milk powder	3 tbsp
3 cups	white flour*	4 cups
2	cloves garlic, minced	3
1/2 tsp	dried rosemary	3/4 tsp
1/4 tsp	pepper	1/2 tsp
1 1/4 tsp	bread-machine or instant yeast	1 1/2 tsp

*In Canada use all-purpose or bread flour; in the United States use bread flour.

1. Add all ingredients to machine according to manufacturer's directions. Select basic white cycle.

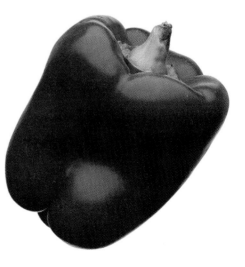

deli rye bread

Use thin slices of this dense-textured, moist bread for open-faced Rueben sandwiches. Since the sauerkraut is already in the bread, just top it with corned beef or pastrami, mustard and Swiss cheese and bake. Even people who don't like sauerkraut as an accompaniment will love the flavor.

LARGE	INGREDIENTS	EXTRA LARGE
3/4 cup	water	1 cup
1 1/4 cup	sauerkraut, well drained and lightly packed	1 1/2 cups
2 tbsp	vegetable oil, margarine or butter	3 tbsp
3/4 tsp	salt	1 tsp
3 tbsp	molasses	1/4 cup
1 cup	white flour*	1 1/2 cups
1 cup	whole-wheat flour	1 3/4 cups
1 1/3 cups	rye flour**	1 1/2 cups
1/2 tsp	pepper	3/4 tsp
1 tbsp	dill or caraway seeds	1 1/2 tbsp
1 tbsp	flaxseed	1 1/2 tbsp
1 1/4 tsp	bread-machine or instant yeast	1 1/2 tsp

*In Canada use all-purpose or bread flour; in the United States use bread flour.
**In the United States add gluten flour: 2 tbsp for a large loaf, or 3 tbsp for an extra-large loaf. (See Gluten, page 147.) In Canada you may wish to substitute a specialty blend of rye flour and enriched wheat flour for the white and rye flours.

1. Select loaf size. Add all ingredients to machine according to manufacturer's directions. Select whole-wheat cycle (if available) or basic white cycle.

roasted garlic bread

You'll be able to enjoy the aroma of roasted garlic twice: once while roasting it and again while the bread bakes! Roasted garlic has a more mellow flavor than raw garlic so don't be alarmed at the quantity. I like to roast about six bulbs of garlic at a time and refrigerate or freeze the extra for future use. This bread makes a great roast-beef sandwich and it's also good with salads.

TIP
To roast garlic, cut the tops off whole, unpeeled bulbs of garlic, exposing the cloves. Wrap in foil and roast at 400°F for 45 to 50 minutes or until soft. Cool, then squeeze softened cloves out of skins. One head yields about 2 to 3 tbsp mashed garlic.

VARIATIONS
Substitute 1 tsp Italian seasoning for rosemary, basil and thyme.
Use 1 to 2 large cloves minced garlic, if you don't have time to roast garlic.

LARGE	INGREDIENTS	EXTRA LARGE
1 1/4 cups	water	1 1/2 cups
3 tbsp	mashed roasted garlic (see Tip)	1/4 cup
1 tbsp	olive oil or vegetable oil	2 tbsp
3/4 tsp	salt	1 tsp
2 tsp	sugar	1 tbsp
3 1/4 cups	white flour*	4 cups
1/2 tsp	dried rosemary	3/4 tsp
1/4 tsp	each dried basil and thyme	1/4 tsp
1 1/4 tsp	bread-machine or instant yeast	1 1/2 tsp

*In Canada use all-purpose or bread flour; in the United States use bread flour.

1. Add all ingredients to machine according to manufacturer's directions. Select basic white cycle.

savory sweet potato bread

TIPS

Leftover sweet potatoes can be mixed with mashed potatoes for a superb colorful vegetable side dish or frozen for later use. Substitute fresh cooked, mashed sweet potatoes and their cooking water for the canned sweet potatoes and reserved liquid. Add a little more sugar if desired. For a lighter texture, substitute 1 large egg for 1/4 cup of the reserved liquid.

VARIATION
Clover Leaf Rolls
Select dough cycle. When cycle is complete, remove dough to lightly floured surface, cover, and let rest for 5 to 10 minutes. Shape as directed for variation of Cheddar Rolls (page 105).

My good friend and home economist Joyce George told me that one of her favorite recipes for dinner rolls included sweet potatoes and a hint of nutmeg. This bread is an adaptation of her recipe and the clover leaf rolls are terrific with ham or turkey or for potluck dinners. With its subtle sweetness, hint of spice and glorious color, this bread is wonderful for ham and onion or spicy crab sandwiches. Canned sweet potatoes or yams are more convenient and you can use the reserved liquid to add extra flavor.

LARGE	INGREDIENTS	EXTRA LARGE
1 cup	mashed, canned sweet potatoes or yams (drained, reserve liquid)	1 1/3 cup
1/2 cup	reserved liquid from sweet potatoes or yams	3/4 cup
2 tbsp	vegetable oil, margarine or butter	3 tbsp
3/4 tsp	salt	1 tsp
1 tbsp	sugar	2 tbsp
3 cups	white flour*	4 cups
1/4 tsp	pepper, nutmeg or dried chili peppers	1/2 tsp
1 1/4 tsp	bread-machine or instant yeast	1 1/2 tsp

*In Canada use all-purpose or bread flour; in the United States use bread flour.

1. Add all ingredients to machine according to manufacturer's directions. Select basic white cycle.

tomato-pepper bread

Tomatoes give this light-textured bread a fabulous color and flavor as well as adding nutrients. Vary the amount of pepper or substitute red or green hot pepper sauce to taste. This loaf makes great club, roast beef, chicken or bacon sandwiches, and you can serve the spicier version with Italian or Mexican meals. Broil thick squares to make crostini, then spread with chèvre or cream cheese and top with pesto or tapenade for a tasty snack.

TIPS

In Canada I recommend using only all-purpose flour for this recipe because the acidity of the tomatoes gives this bread a very tender, light texture and increased volume.

A 14-oz can of tomatoes is sufficient for the extra-large loaf.

LARGE	INGREDIENTS	EXTRA LARGE
1 1/3 cups	canned tomatoes (including liquid), broken up with spoon	1 3/4 cups
2 tbsp	vegetable or olive oil	3 tbsp
3/4 tsp	salt	1 tsp
1 tbsp	brown sugar, packed	2 tbsp
1/4 tsp	pepper or dried chili peppers	1/2 tsp
3 cups	white flour*	4 cups
1 tsp	bread-machine or instant yeast	1 1/4 tsp

*In Canada use all-purpose flour; in the United States use bread flour.

VARIATIONS

Add 1 to 2 tsp dried rosemary, basil or Italian seasoning.

Substitute 1 to 1 1/2 tsp black sesame seeds for the pepper.

1. Add all ingredients to machine according to manufacturer's directions. Select basic white bread cycle.

carrot ginger bread

This colorful and tasty loaf is packed full of nutrients. Serve it as an accompaniment to curried dishes and soups or use it for curried tuna or chicken sandwiches.

The beet variation would be great for April Fools' Day (everyone will think it is cranberry). It is wonderful with stews and cabbage soup, or for Danish open-faced sandwiches topped with shaved beef or herring. Eating these breads is a great way to get more vegetables into our diets.

TIPS
This bread has no sugar; the yeast feeds on the natural sweetness of the vegetables.
These doughs will be dry at first and then will become moister. Since the moisture content of the vegetables can vary throughout the year, check the dough at the ingredient signal (or about 20 to 30 minutes into the cycle) and adjust the consistency if necessary.
Wrap leftover gingerroot and freeze; it grates easily while frozen.

VARIATION
Beet and Horseradish or Dill Bread
Substitute grated beets for the carrots. For large loaf, substitute 1 tsp vinegar and 1 tbsp horseradish for the gingerroot. For an extra-large loaf, use 2 tsp vinegar and 1 1/2 tbsp horseradish. You can also use 2 to 3 tsp dried dillweed instead of the horseradish.

LARGE	INGREDIENTS	EXTRA LARGE
2/3 cup	water	3/4 cup
1 tbsp	vegetable oil	1 tbsp
2 cups (about 7 oz)	lightly packed grated carrot	2 1/2 cups (about 8 oz)
1 tsp	salt	1 1/4 tsp
1 tbsp	grated gingerroot	1 1/2 tbsp
2 tbsp	dried onion flakes	3 tbsp
3 cups	white flour*	4 cups
1 1/4 tsp	bread-machine or instant yeast	1 1/2 tsp

*In Canada use all-purpose or bread flour; in the United States use bread flour.

1. Add all ingredients to machine according to manufacturer's directions. Select basic white bread cycle.

chapter four

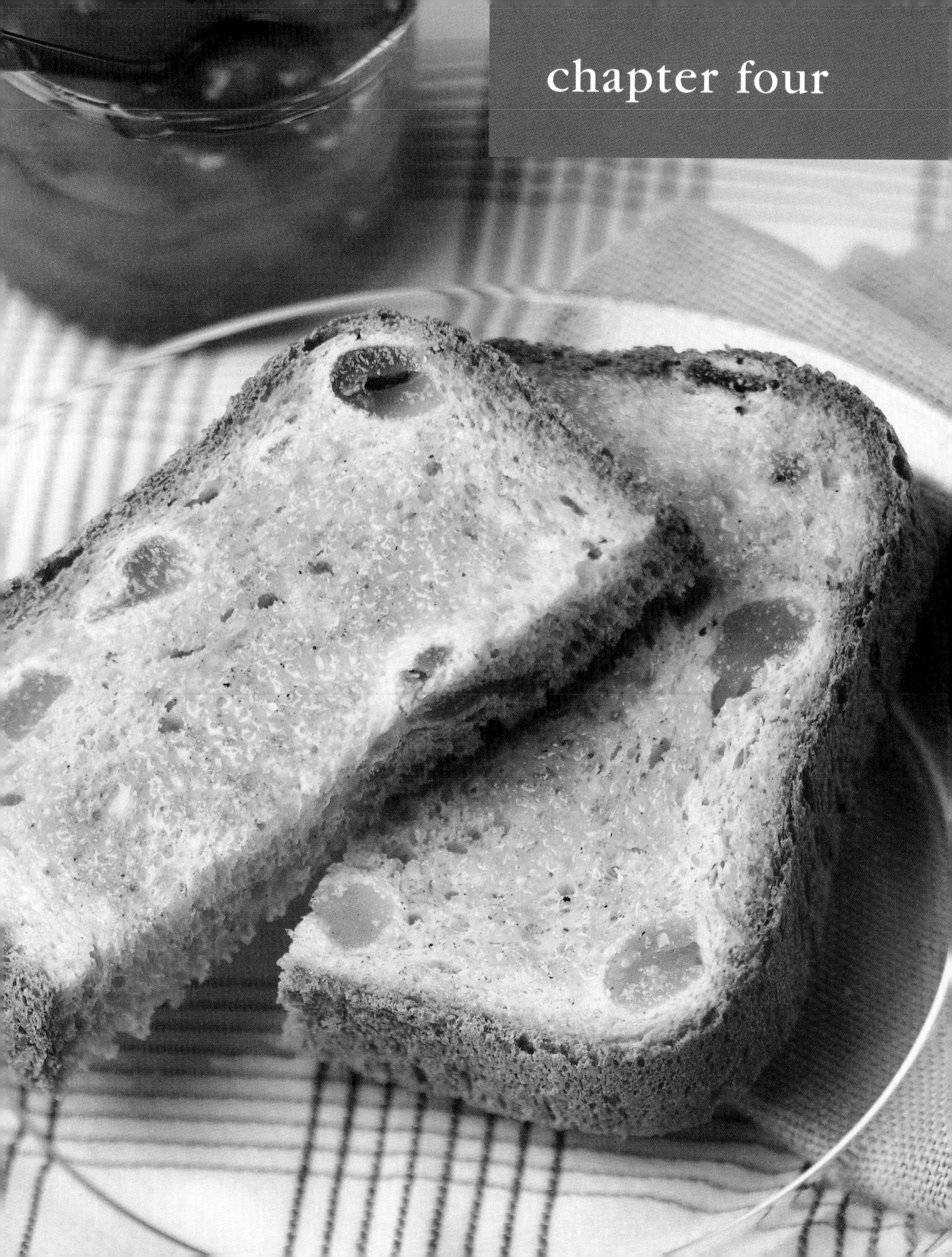

The breads in this chapter are all made in the bread machine and are a welcome addition to breakfasts, brunches, coffee parties or afternoon tea. The fragrance and flavor of sweet spices such as cinnamon, nutmeg, ginger and anise seed are teamed up with a variety of fruits including banana, apricots, mangoes or pumpkin. The blend of chocolate and cherry in the Black Forest Bread makes for a great dessert. There is also a more basic but popular Cinnamon–raisin Bread in chapter 2 (a variation of Honey 'n' Wheat English-muffin Bread).

Dried fruits add a heartier texture to loaves such as Panettone while canned or fresh fruits add moisture. Oatmeal, whole wheat, bran, wheat germ and spelt are also used in some of these recipes to add nutrients, fiber and texture as well as a more complex dimension of taste.

blueberry swirl sour-cream bread

maple walnut bread

caribbean banana bread

black forest bread

tropical fruit and coconut bread

double pumpkin, cranberry and raisin bread

spiced pear and hazelnut bread

double ginger and oatmeal bread

spiced apricot and oatmeal bread

panettone

ancient grain, seed and fruit loaf

blueberry swirl sour-cream bread

My colleague and friend Sue Bailey has developed so many muffin recipes in her career that we often call her the "Muffin Queen." One of her favorites that I enjoyed on a cross-country ski getaway inspired this recipe. Even before the recipe was perfected, everyone who tasted the bread wanted a copy of the recipe right away! The moist, dense texture of this loaf is more like a tea bread than a yeast bread. Enjoy it for breakfast, brunch or dessert and since blueberries contain antioxidants, it's good for you too!

LARGE	INGREDIENTS	EXTRA LARGE
1/3 cup	light sour cream	1/2 cup
2/3 cup	low-fat milk	3/4 cup
3 tbsp	margarine or butter	1/4 cup
1	large egg(s)	2
1 1/2 tsp	grated lemon or orange rind	2 tsp
1/2 tsp	each salt and baking soda	3/4 tsp
1/4 cup	brown sugar, packed	1/3 cup
3 cups	white flour*	4 cups
3/4 tsp	ground cinnamon	1 tsp
1 1/4 tsp	bread-machine or instant yeast	1 1/4 tsp
3/4 cup	fresh or frozen blueberries	1 cup

*In Canada use all-purpose or bread flour; in the United States use bread flour.

1. Add all ingredients except blueberries to machine according to manufacturer's directions. Select sweet or basic white cycle.

2. Add fresh or frozen blueberries at ingredient signal (or about 20 to 30 minutes into cycle). Don't be alarmed when the dough becomes quite soft and sticky after you add the berries.

maple walnut bread

In the spring when I was growing up, Mom often served ice cream drizzled with maple syrup and topped with walnuts. Maple-walnut became my favorite ice-cream flavor and just recently, on a culinary trip to Montreal, I enjoyed the same flavors in a yeast bread. My version, with a little bran added for fiber, makes an excellent breakfast bread. Enjoy it with Quebec, Ontario or Vermont maple syrup.

TIPS
California walnuts are sweeter and less bitter than other varieties.

If you will be away from the machine at the ingredient signal, add the nuts at the beginning of the cycle, but use large pieces of nuts so that they won't be pulverized during the kneading.

LARGE	INGREDIENTS	EXTRA LARGE
3/4 cup	water	1 cup
1/2 cup	maple syrup	3/4 cup
2 tbsp	margarine, butter or vegetable oil	3 tbsp
1/2 tsp	salt	3/4 tsp
3 tbsp	instant skim-milk powder	1/4 cup
2 3/4 cups	white flour*	3 3/4 cups
1/3 cup	bakers' natural bran	2/3 cup
1 tsp	bread-machine or instant yeast	1 1/4 tsp
3/4 cup	California walnut pieces	1 cup

*In Canada use all-purpose flour or bread flour; in the United States use bread flour.

VARIATION
For large loaf use 1/2 cup nuts and add 1/4 cup raisins; for extra-large loaf use 3/4 cup nuts and 1/2 cup raisins.

1. Add all ingredients except nuts to machine according to manufacturer's directions. Select basic white cycle.

2. Add nuts at ingredient signal (or about 20 to 30 minutes into cycle).

caribbean banana bread

When my children were growing up they loved the banana muffins that a long-time friend Marion Philips used to make. Her recipe had lots of nutmeg. In this recipe, you can substitute cinnamon for the nutmeg. Bananas should be very ripe for the best flavor and the most moisture.

TIP
Freeze overripe bananas either in their skins (the skins will turn black but the bananas are good for baking when thawed) or peel, mash and freeze in airtight containers or bags.

LARGE	INGREDIENTS	EXTRA LARGE
1/3 cup	water	1/3 cup
3/4 cup	mashed ripe banana	1 cup
2 tbsp	vegetable oil, margarine or butter	3 tbsp
1	large egg(s)	2
3/4 tsp	salt	1 tsp
3 tbsp	brown sugar, packed	1/4 cup
1 1/2 cups	white flour*	2 cups
1 1/2 cups	whole-wheat flour	2 cups
1 tsp	ground nutmeg or cinnamon	1 1/4 tsp
1 1/4 tsp	bread-machine or instant yeast	1 1/2 tsp
1/4 cup	each raisins and chopped pecans (optional)	1/3 cup

*In Canada use all-purpose or bread flour; in the United States use bread flour.

1. Add all ingredients except raisins and nuts to machine according to manufacturer's directions. Select sweet or basic white cycle.
2. Add raisins and nuts at ingredient signal (or about 20 to 30 minutes into cycle after the starting time).

black forest bread

TIP

Jumbo chocolate chips won't melt as fast as regular-size chips. If the chips don't totally melt, the kneading action of your machine may produce nice pockets of chocolate. Leftover Black Forest Bread would make a wonderful chocolate bread pudding.

This chocoholic's fantasy combines the chocolate and cherry flavors of the famous cake. Although maraschino cherries are not always my favorite, they are the perfect choice for this recipe because, in addition to their attractive appearance, they provide moisture and sweetness. Serve this bread at brunch or afternoon coffee, or cut it in squares and top it with whipped mascarpone or cream cheese and toasted almonds for dessert.

LARGE	INGREDIENTS	EXTRA LARGE
1 cup	water	1 1/4 cups
2 tbsp	margarine, butter or vegetable oil	3 tbsp
1	large egg	1
1/2 tsp	salt	3/4 tsp
1 tsp	almond or vanilla extract	2 tsp
1/4 cup	sugar	1/3 cup
3 cups	white flour*	4 cups
3 tbsp	instant skim-milk powder	1/4 cup
3 tbsp	unsweetened cocoa powder	1/4 cup
1 1/4 tsp	bread-machine yeast or instant yeast	1 1/4 tsp
2/3 cup	semi-sweet chocolate chips	1 cup
1/3 cup	whole maraschino cherries, well drained on paper towel	2/3 cup

*In Canada use all-purpose or bread flour; in the United States use bread flour.

1. Add all ingredients except chocolate chips and cherries to machine according to manufacturer's directions. Select sweet or basic white cycle.

2. Add chocolate chips and cherries at ingredient signal (or about 20 to 30 minutes into cycle).

tropical fruit and coconut bread

This loaf is reminiscent of a quick bread we had for breakfast in Hawaii. Mangoes and papayas are equally good in this recipe, but papaya gives a stronger color. Since the recipe uses canned fruit, this bread can be made at any time of year. Mangoes are rich in vitamins A, C and D while papaya is a good source of vitamins A and C.

TIP
A 14-oz can of fruit is sufficient for an extra-large loaf; leftover fruit is terrific in milkshakes or fruit salads.

VARIATIONS
If mango or papaya is not available, you can substitute canned tropical fruit mix or pineapple, but the bread will have a milder flavor and a lighter color.

Substitute puréed ripe fresh fruit for the canned fruit, and fruit nectar diluted with water for the reserved liquid.

LARGE	INGREDIENTS	EXTRA LARGE
3/4 cup	puréed canned mango or papaya (drain liquid and reserve)	1 cup
1/2 cup	reserved liquid from mango or papaya	3/4 cup
2 tbsp	vegetable oil, margarine or butter	3 tbsp
1 1/2 tsp	grated lime rind	2 tsp
1/4 tsp	rum or vanilla extract (optional)	1/2 tsp
3/4 tsp	salt	1 tsp
1 tbsp	sugar	2 tbsp
3 cups	white flour*	4 cups
1 1/4 tsp	bread-machine or instant yeast	1 1/2 tsp
1/3 cup	shredded or flaked unsweetened coconut	1/2 cup
1/4 cup	diced dried mango or papaya (optional)	1/3 cup

*In Canada use all-purpose or bread flour; in the United States use bread flour.

1. Add all ingredients to machine according to manufacturer's directions. Select sweet or basic white cycle.

double pumpkin, cranberry and raisin bread

The Native peoples were the first to cultivate squash and pumpkin and they used these vegetables in breads made with cornmeal. They also taught us how to tap maple trees to make maple syrup. This yummy autumn bread is subtly sweetened with maple syrup and the pumpkin seeds (pepitas) give it a crunchy texture. Make it in the bread machine or transfer the dough to tall cans and bake it in the oven. This bread makes a beautiful hostess gift.

LARGE	INGREDIENTS	EXTRA LARGE
2 tbsp	water	3 tbsp
1 cup	canned pumpkin purée	1 1/4 cups
3 tbsp	margarine, butter or vegetable oil	1/4 cup
1 /2 tsp	salt	3/4 tsp
1	large egg	1
3 tbsp	maple syrup	1/4 cup
3 cups	white flour*	4 cups
1 tsp	ground cinnamon	1 1/2 tsp
1/2 tsp	ground nutmeg	3/4 tsp
1 tsp	bread-machine or instant yeast	1 1/4 tsp
1/3 cup	unsalted pumpkin seeds	1/2 cup
1/2 cup	fresh or frozen whole cranberries	2/3 cup
1/2 cup	raisins	2/3 cup

*In Canada use all-purpose or bread flour; in the United States use bread flour.

VARIATIONS

Substitute slivered almonds for the pumpkin seeds.

Oven-baked Cylindrical Loaf
Select dough cycle. Meanwhile grease a 48-oz juice can and line bottom and sides with parchment paper so that the paper extends 1/2 inch past the top. When cycle is complete, remove dough to lightly floured surface, cover and let rest 5 to 10 minutes.

Shape dough into a smooth round ball, place in can, cover and let rise about 30 to 40 minutes or until the can is about 3/4 full. Bake at 375°F for 40 minutes or until the crust is golden brown (or an instant-read thermometer inserted in center reads 200°F). If necessary, cover with foil during last 5 to10 minutes to prevent over-browning.

1. Add all ingredients except pumpkin seeds, cranberries and raisins to machine according to manufacturer's directions. Select sweet or basic white cycle.

2. Add seeds, cranberries and raisins at ingredient signal (or about 20 to 30 minutes into the cycle).

spiced pear and hazelnut bread

I first tasted warm pear bread in France at breakfast. Pears add vitamin C and fiber to this loaf. The mace accents the subtle pear flavor while the hazelnuts provide a sweet, rich flavor and texture. Mace (the outer covering of the nutmeg seed) has a slightly more pungent flavor than nutmeg but nutmeg can be substituted if mace is not available.

LARGE	INGREDIENTS	EXTRA LARGE
3/4 cup	puréed canned pears in juice (drain juice and reserve)	1 1/4 cups
1/2 cup	reserved juice from pears	2/3 cup
1/4 tsp	vanilla or brandy extract	1/2 tsp
1 tbsp	margarine or butter	2 tbsp
1 tbsp	sugar	2 tbsp
1/4 tsp	mace	1/2 tsp
3/4 tsp	salt	1 tsp
3 cups	white flour*	4 cups
1 1/4 tsp	bread-machine or instant yeast	1 1/2 tsp
1/3 cup	coarsely chopped hazelnuts	1/2 cup

*In Canada use all-purpose or bread flour; in the United States use bread flour.

1. Add all ingredients to machine according to manufacturer's directions. Select sweet or basic white cycle.

double ginger and oatmeal bread

The flavors of this loaf were inspired by a favorite cookie. Candied or crystallized ginger is made by cooking ginger in a sugar syrup and coating it with coarse sugar. The dates add a contrasting darker color and a rich sweetness to blend with the peppery, slightly sweet ginger. The rolled oats contribute fiber and help to keep the bread fresh.

A number of years ago my dear English friend Betty Wright introduced me to ginger and cream cheese sandwiches; now I cut this bread into fancy shapes for cream cheese sandwiches.

TIPS
Because instant oats have been partially cooked during processing, they are not interchangeable with either quick-cooking or old-fashioned rolled oats. Do not use instant oats in this recipe.

If you use preserved ginger or stem ginger, drain off all the syrup and dry the ginger thoroughly with paper towel.

The easiest way to chop dates, ginger or other dried fruit is to use scissors. When the scissors get sticky, run the blades under hot water.

For fancy sandwiches, use small cookie cutters to cut shapes from slices of bread. Spread with cream cheese; serve open face topped with nuts, jam or grapes. Use any left-over scraps to make a delicious bread pudding.

VARIATION
Substitute raisins or chopped prunes for the dates.

LARGE	INGREDIENTS	EXTRA LARGE
1 1/4 cups	water	1 1/2 cups
2 tbsp	margarine, butter or vegetable oil	3 tbsp
3/4 tsp	salt	1 tsp
3 tbsp	sugar	1/4 cup
3 tbsp	instant skim-milk powder	1/4 cup
2 3/4 cup	white flour*	3 1/4 cups
1/2 cup	quick-cooking rolled oats	3/4 cup
2 tsp	ground ginger	1 tbsp
1/4 cup	chopped crystallized ginger	1/3 cup
1 1/4 tsp	bread-machine or instant yeast	1 1/2 tsp
1/2 cup	chopped dates (optional)	3/4 cup

*In Canada use all-purpose or bread flour; in the United States use bread flour.

1. Add all ingredients except dates to machine according to manufacturer's directions. Select sweet or basic white cycle.
2. Add dates at ingredient signal (or about 20 to 30 minutes into cycle).

spiced apricot and oatmeal bread

This nourishing bread is wonderful as a snack with afternoon tea or toasted for breakfast. If you have the time, make the braided variation for an attractive brunch centerpiece.

Rolled oats (or oatmeal) is made by steaming oat groats, then rolling them into flakes. For quick-cooking rolled oats, the groats are cut into several pieces before being steamed and rolled. Breads made with oatmeal have more fiber and they also stay fresh longer. The wheat germ in this recipe adds nutritional value as well as a nutty flavor.

TIPS
It's easier to cut apricots with scissors than to chop them with a knife.

One average orange yields about 2 tsp grated rind.

VARIATION
Braided Loaf
Select dough cycle. When cycle is complete, remove dough to lightly floured surface; cover and let rest 5 to 10 minutes. Divide dough into 3 pieces and roll each piece into a 13-inch rope. Place on greased baking sheet. To braid: bring left rope under center rope and lay it down, then bring right rope under new center rope and lay it down. Repeat to end. Pinch ends together to seal and tuck under braid.

Cover, let rise in warm place until doubled in bulk, about 45 minutes.

Beat 1 egg with 1 tbsp water and brush on braid. Bake at 375°F for 25 to 30 minutes or crust is golden brown or an instant-read thermometer inserted in center reads 200°F. Cool on rack. If desired sift confectioners' sugar on top or decorate with frosting for Panettone (see Variations, page 77).

LARGE	INGREDIENTS	EXTRA LARGE
1 cup	water	1 1/3 cups
2 tbsp	margarine, butter or vegetable oil	3 tbsp
3/4 tsp	salt	1 tsp
1	large egg	1
2 tbsp	honey	3 tbsp
2 tsp	grated orange rind	1 tbsp
3 cups	white flour*	4 cups
1/2 cup	quick-cooking rolled oats	3/4 cup
1 1/2 tbsp	wheat germ (optional)	2 tbsp
1 1/4 tsp	bread-machine or instant yeast	1 1/2 tsp
1 tsp	ground nutmeg	1 1/4 tsp
2/3 cup	coarsely chopped dried apricots	1 cup

*In Canada use all-purpose or bread flour; in the United States use bread flour.

1. Add all ingredients except apricots to machine according to manufacturer's directions. Select basic white bread cycle.

2. Add apricots at ingredient signal (or about 20 to 30 minutes into kneading cycle).

panettone

The traditional version of this classic Italian Christmas bread is shaped like a dome — similar to the shape of a loaf made in a round or vertical bread-machine pan. For a true Italian touch make it with rum. If desired frost and decorate with peel. When we were in Italy my Italian friend Gisella Isadore cut the top off, hollowed out the center, sprinkled it with orange liqueur and packed the loaf with ice cream to serve as dessert. Use scooped-out bread for bread pudding.

VARIATIONS

Substitute 2 tbsp rum for 2 tbsp water and omit extract.

For a frosted loaf, combine 1/2 cup confectioners' sugar, 2 tsp softened butter or margarine, 2 tsp orange or lemon juice and 1 tsp grated orange or lemon rind; mix until smooth. Spread on cooled loaf and decorate with candied peel if desired.

Oven-baked Loaves

Use 19- to 28-oz food cans or 2-lb coffee cans.

Select extra-large loaf and dough cycle. Meanwhile grease cans and line bottom and sides with parchment paper, allowing the paper to extend 1 inch above the top of can. When cycle is complete, remove dough to lightly floured surface; cover and let rest 5 to 10 minutes.

Fill cans half full with a smooth round ball of dough. Wrap outside of cans with double layer of foil. Cover and let rise in a warm place 35 to 75 minutes or until doubled in size.

Bake at 350°F on bottom rack of oven for 30 to 60 minutes or until crust is golden brown and sounds hollow when tapped. Cool completely on rack. Remove from cans.

LARGE	INGREDIENTS	EXTRA LARGE
1/2 cup	water	3/4 cup
2 tbsp	margarine, butter or vegetable oil	3 tbsp
2	large eggs	2 plus 1 yolk
1/2 tsp	rum or vanilla extract	1 tsp
3/4 tsp	salt	3/4 tsp
1/4 cup	sugar	1/3 cup
2 tbsp	instant skim-milk powder	3 tbsp
1 tsp	each grated lemon and orange rind	1 tsp
1/2 tsp	anise seeds	3/4 tsp
2 1/2 cups	white flour*	3 cups
1 1/4 tsp	bread machine or instant yeast	1 1/4 tsp
2 tbsp	each diced candied orange and citron peel	3 tbsp
1/4 cup	each golden raisins and toasted slivered almonds	1/3 cup

*In Canada use all-purpose or bread flour; in the United States use bread flour.

1. Add all ingredients except peel, raisins and almonds to machine according to manufacturer's directions. Select sweet or basic white cycle.

2. Add fruits and nuts at ingredient signal (or about 20 to 30 minutes into cycle).

If desired, brush the finished loaf with melted butter for a softer crust and sprinkle with sugar.

apple and cornmeal bread

The idea for this flavor combination came from my dear friend and assistant Bev Watson, who tasted it in a restaurant on the West Coast with her daughter Kim. This version is a variation of Anadama bread, a classic New England favorite made with molasses and cornmeal. Use concentrated apple juice in place of water for a stronger flavor. This is not an overly sweet bread and has a dense texture so is terrific for ham, pork or grilled cheese sandwiches and makes a pleasant change from plain white bread for breakfast toast.

TIPS
To measure honey more easily, heat the jar for a few seconds in the microwave. If you measure honey in the same spoon you used for the oil it will slide off the spoon easily.

Substitute apple juice for frozen concentrate and water.

LARGE	INGREDIENTS	EXTRA LARGE
1/3 cup	frozen unsweetened apple juice concentrate, thawed	1/2 cup
2/3 cup	water	3/4 cup
2 tbsp	vegetable oil, margarine or butter	3 tbsp
3/4 tsp	salt	1 tsp
1 tbsp	honey or maple syrup	2 tbsp
2 cups	white flour*	2 3/4 cups
3/4 cup	cornmeal	1 cup
1 1/4 tsp	bread-machine or instant yeast	1 1/2 tsp

*In Canada use all-purpose or bread flour; in the United States use bread flour.

1. Add all ingredients to machine according to manufacturer's directions. Select basic white bread cycle.

ancient grain, seed and fruit loaf

TIP

The easiest way to chop figs or other dried fruit is to cut with scissors. When the scissors get sticky, run the blades under hot water.

The three main ingredients in this interesting loaf were first used thousands of years ago and they all have impressive nutrient values. Spelt is a high-protein grain that will grow in harsh conditions; it was used extensively until 200 years ago and is now making a comeback. Because spelt is low in gluten, I have combined it with wheat flour for a lighter loaf. Figs have a higher fiber, mineral and calcium content than most other fruits and they also add a special flavor. Anise seed lends a pleasant perfume and sweet licorice flavor.

LARGE	INGREDIENTS	EXTRA LARGE
1 cup	water	1 1/3 cups
2 tbsp	margarine, butter or vegetable oil	3 tbsp
1	large egg	1
3/4 tsp	salt	1 tsp
3 tbsp	brown sugar, packed	1/4 cup
2 cups	white flour*	3 cups
1 1/4 cups	whole-grain spelt flour	1 1/2 cups
1 tbsp	anise seed	4 tsp
1 1/4 tsp	bread-machine or instant yeast	1 1/4 tsp
1/2 cup	coarsely chopped dried figs	2/3 cup

*In Canada use all-purpose or bread flour; in the United States use bread flour.

1. Add all ingredients except figs to machine according to manufacturer's directions. Select whole wheat cycle.

2. Add figs at ingredient signal (or about 20 to 30 minutes into the cycle).

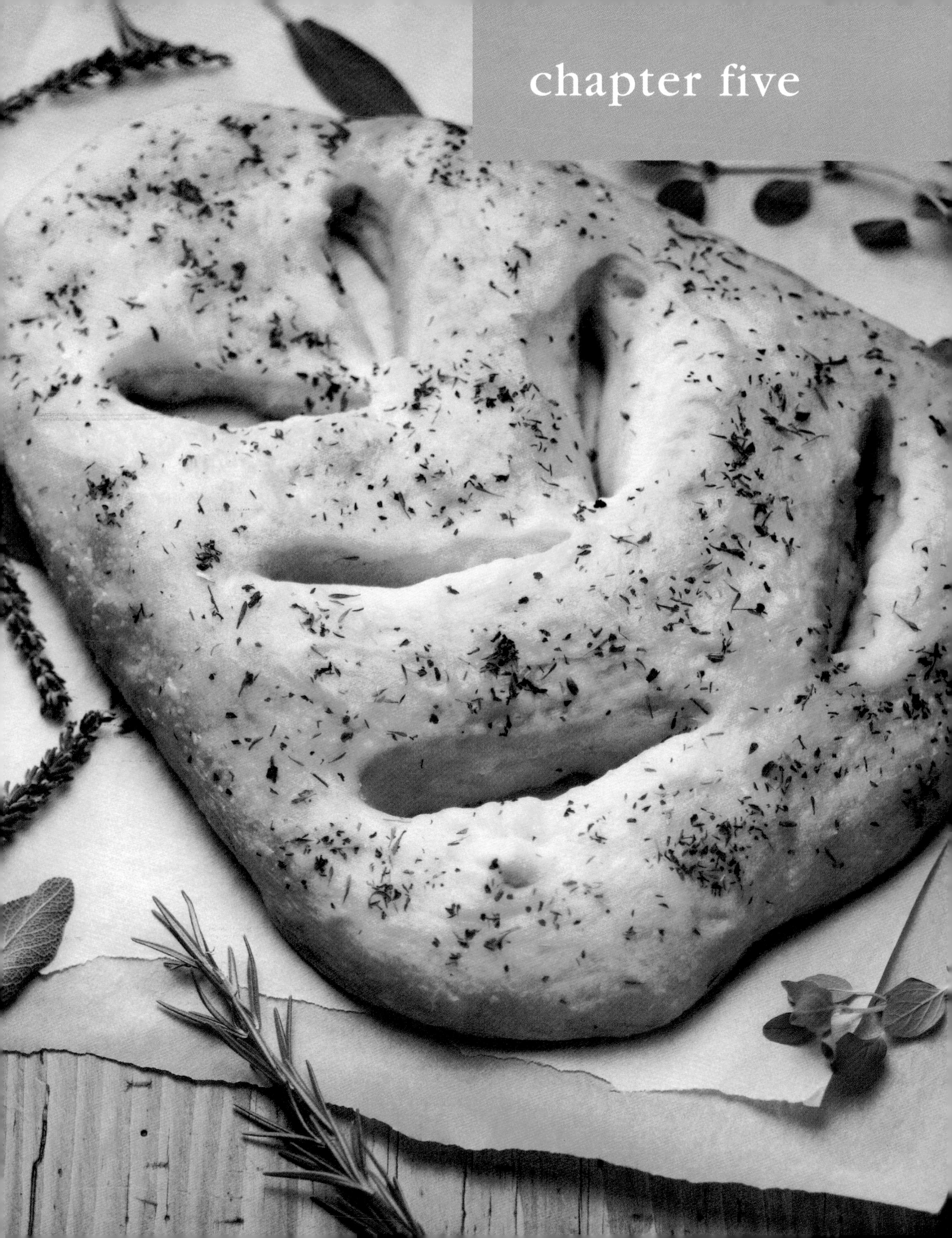

chapter five

All the flatbreads in this global collection are shaped from dough made in the bread machine. Some — such as pizza, calzone and foccacia — will be familiar, while others — such as fougasse and galettes — may be new discoveries for you.

There are five different pizza doughs to choose from. Making pizza is a wonderful way to introduce hungry family members to the bread machine. The dough is so easy to make and so much more economical than purchased dough, and with the delay-start timer the dough will be ready when you are! Let the children make a pizza with the more traditional toppings (page 87), then try some of the more creative recipes (such as Carmelized Onion and Three Cheese or Potato, Red Onion and Sage) for the adults. You can even use pizza dough to create edible bowls for salads and chili con carne.

Main course breads for brunch, lunch or supper (such as Broccoli and Chicken Calzone, Pizza Rustica, Mediterranean Stuffed Buns and Galettes) are also great for "meals on the go." I hope you find the fun of creating these global recipes as satisfying as your family and friends will find eating the results.

pizza

TIPS

I find it easier to spread dough on perforated pizza pans. Perforated pans and pizza stones also give a crispier crust.
Place a damp cloth under the pizza pan to prevent movement while shaping.

Storage for Pizza Dough
Seal and refrigerate unrisen dough up to one day.
Seal and freeze unrisen dough up to two months; thaw up to 12 hours ahead of time for 2 1/2 hours at room temperature or overnight in refrigerator.
To prebake crusts, prick them with a fork and bake at 450°F for 10 to 12 minutes. Cool on racks, wrap in foil to seal and freeze for up to two weeks.

According to Neapolitans, the pizza made in Naples, Italy, is the original and it cannot be duplicated anywhere. Neapolitan pizzas have a thin crust and the only toppings are local tomatoes, seasonings, mozzarella cheese and olive oil. They are served whole for individual meals, cut in wedges to be shared before main courses or folded over like a book and eaten as a snack.

However, pizzas in other areas of Italy and in many other countries have thicker crusts, more substantial toppings and even double crusts. Today there are no hard and fast rules for pizza crusts, filling or toppings. Calzone combines the familiar fillings and flavors of pizza with the convenience of a sandwich. Pizza Rustica is a deep, layered double-crusted pizza. You can use my recipe suggestions or let your imagination flow and create new flavor combinations (as my son Brent does) with whatever ingredients are on hand.

The beauty of making pizza dough in the bread machine is that you can use the delay-start timer to have dough ready when you come home from school or work. If you don't use all the dough, you can refrigerate or freeze it for later use. (See page 150 for tips on storing dough.)

Shaping and Baking Pizza Doughs
For 2 12-inch thin-crust pizzas, divide dough in half. Push and pat each piece of dough into a lightly greased 12-inch pizza pan. For 1 thicker oval crust pizza, press dough onto prepared baking sheet. For 8 individual pizzas, divide dough into 8 pieces, press into 5-inch circles and place on prepared baking sheet. The prepared pans can be also sprinkled with cornmeal to prevent sticking. If the dough seems too elastic, let it rest a few minutes.

For thin-crust pizzas add toppings immediately. For pizzas with a slightly thicker crust, allow the dough to rise in a warm place for about 20 to 30 minutes, then add toppings. Bake pizzas at 450°F on bottom shelf of oven for 15 to 20 minutes or as directed in recipe.

Grilled or Barbecued Pizzas
Prepare dough as directed above and place on cornmeal-lined pans; keep cold until ready to grill. Gently lift crusts onto lightly oiled grill, cornmeal side down. Grill about 3 minutes, rotating occasionally, or until the bottom is golden and the top is puffy. Turn crust grilled side up, prick 2 or 3 times with a fork and spread on toppings. Cover and grill 4 to 5 minutes or until crust is browned and cheese is melted.

basic pizza dough

This basic dough provides a versatile base for any of your favorite toppings. However, the cornmeal changes the texture, so you may want to try the Traditional Pizza Dough as well. The Multigrain Pizza Dough is a terrific way to add more fiber to your diet, and the No-fat Cornmeal Pizza Dough is excellent for Mexican toppings. Finally, use your favorite pizza dough to make edible bread bowls for a unique presentation of salads or chili — this super idea is from my friend and colleague, Sue Bailey.

YIELD: 2 12-inch thin-crust pizzas, 1 oval thick-crust pizza, 8 5-inch individual pizzas or 2 12- x 7-inch oblong pizzas.

INGREDIENTS

1 1/4 cups	water
2 tbsp	olive or vegetable oil
3/4 tsp	salt
3 cups	white flour*
1/3 cup	cornmeal
1 1/2 tsp	bread-machine yeast or instant yeast

*In Canada use all-purpose or bread flour; in the United States use bread flour.

1. Add all ingredients to machine according to manufacturer's directions. Select dough cycle.

2. When cycle is complete, remove dough to lightly floured surface; cover and let rest 5 to 10 minutes. Shape as directed for specific recipes on following pages, or see "Shaping and Baking Pizza Doughs," page 84 or store for later use.

VARIATIONS

Traditional Pizza Dough
Substitute 1/4 cup white flour for the cornmeal.

Multigrain Pizza Dough
Substitute 1 1/2 cups white flour, 1 cup whole-wheat flour and 1/2 cup of a multigrain cereal mix (see Tip page 33) for the flour and cornmeal in basic recipe.

Herbed Pizza Dough
Add 2 tsp Italian seasoning or 1 tsp dried basil and 1/2 tsp each of oregano and thyme to the Traditional Pizza Dough. For variety, add 1/4 cup grated Parmesan cheese and 1 tsp fennel seeds if desired.

No-fat Cornmeal Pizza Dough
Substitute sugar for oil, decrease salt to 1/2 tsp, decrease flour to 2 1/4 cups and increase cornmeal to 1 cup.

Bread Bowls
For thin, crisp salad bowls, cut dough into 8 pieces. For thick chili bowls, cut dough into 6 pieces. Lightly grease the outside of 1-cup custard dishes (approximately 4 1/2 inches wide) or small oven-proof bowls and place them upside down on sturdy baking sheets. Roll each piece of dough into 7-inch circle; drape and press over outside of cup. Bake in 400°F oven for 15 to 20 minutes or until golden brown. Remove bread bowls from cups and cool on wire racks. Line with lettuce leaves for salads or fill with your favorite chili.

tex-mex pizza

Prepared ingredients make this a quick topping for a South-West flavored crust. For a vegetarian version, substitute canned, drained black beans for the chorizo. Try pre-packaged cheese mixtures in nacho or Tex-Mex flavors instead of the Monterey Jack cheese and add 1/2 tsp cumin to the salsa for more flavor.

YIELD: 1 12-inch pizza.

TIP
If you can't find a ripe avocado, substitute prepared guacamole for the avocado and sour cream.

VARIATIONS
Substitute other varieties of sliced or crumbled cooked sausage (such as turkey, chicken or pork) for the chorizo.

Traditional Pizza
Choose 1/2 recipe of any of the pizza doughs (page 85). Substitute pizza sauce for the salsa, sliced fresh mushrooms for the corn, and diced sweet peppers and onion for the coriander. Omit the avocado and sour cream.

INGREDIENTS

1/2 recipe	No-fat Cornmeal Pizza Dough (page 85) in a 12-inch pizza pan
1 cup	thick medium or hot salsa
1 cup	sliced chorizo or pepperoni sausage (about 4 oz)
1 cup	frozen or canned corn kernels, drained
3/4 cup	fresh coriander, cilantro or Italian parsley leaves, torn, divided
1 1/2 cups	shredded Monterey Jack or mozzarella cheese
1	avocado, peeled and sliced (optional)
1/2 cup	low-fat sour cream (optional)

1. Spread salsa on top of dough leaving a 1/2-inch border around outside. Distribute sausage, corn and 1/2 cup coriander leaves evenly on top. Sprinkle cheese over all.

2. Bake at 450°F on lowest shelf of oven for 15 to 20 minutes or until bubbling and hot. Garnish with avocado slices, sour cream (if desired) and remaining coriander leaves.

caramelized onion and three-cheese pizza

VARIATIONS

Substitute dried Italian seasoning for the rosemary, thyme and savory. Substitute low-fat or dry-curd cottage cheese for the ricotta cheese.

Smoked Salmon and Brie Pizza
You can use either smoked salmon or gravlax for this recipe. Gravlax (raw salmon marinated or cured in salt, dill, sugar and pepper) is a Scandinavian delicacy that is usually served with a sweet-sour mustard and dill sauce. Look for it in specialty fish stores or at the fish counter in supermarkets, or make your own. Omit onion mixture and substitute 1/4 cup honey mustard for the cheese mixture. Top with 8 oz sliced brie cheese and bake for 15 to 17 minutes (or until crust is crisp) as directed. Top with 4 to 6 oz thinly sliced or coarsely chopped smoked salmon or gravlax and return to oven about 2 minutes just to warm salmon. Decorate top with fresh dill, lemon-thyme or grated lemon zest.

The sweetness of the caramelized onions provides an interesting contrast to the creamy herbed cheese base, and this pizza makes a terrific vegetarian addition to menus. The smoked salmon (or gravlax) variation has become one of my husband Allan's favorites for a special brunch.
YIELD: 1 12-inch pizza.

INGREDIENTS

1/2 recipe	Basic or Traditional Pizza Dough (page 85) in 12-inch pizza pan
2 tbsp	olive oil
2 cups	thinly sliced onions
1 tbsp	sugar
1 tbsp	balsamic vinegar
1 1/4 cups	light ricotta cheese
1 cup	shredded provolone or mozzarella cheese
1/4 cup	grated Parmesan cheese
1/2 tsp	dried rosemary
1/4 tsp	each dried thyme and savory

1. Allow dough to rest while preparing topping. In large skillet heat oil over medium-high heat; add onion and cook, stirring often, for 5 minutes or until softened and golden brown. Add sugar and continue cooking for 3 to 4 minutes. Stir in balsamic vinegar and remove from heat to cool slightly. In small bowl, combine ricotta, provolone and Parmesan cheese with rosemary, thyme and savory.

2. Spread cheese mixture on pizza dough, leaving 1/2 -inch border around outside.
3. Bake at 450°F on lowest shelf of oven for 12 minutes. Top with onions and continue to bake 3 to 5 minutes or until crust is browned.

potato, red onion and sage pizza

Sounds strange, but try it — you'll like it! In fact this pizza has become my assistant Bev Watson's favorite and she has converted her nieces and nephews as well. In the Puglia region of Italy, potatoes and other vegetables are used often for economy. My Italian friend Gisella Isadore introduced me to potatoes with sage, but you can use thyme or rosemary if preferred.
YIELD: 1 12-inch pizza

TIPS
3 to 4 medium potatoes yield 3 cups of sliced potatoes.
If substituting ground sage, use about 1/2 tsp.

VARIATION
Substitute 1/2 cup grated Parmesan or Asiago cheese for the creamy cheeses.

INGREDIENTS

1/2 recipe	Basic or Herbed Pizza Dough (page 85) in 12-inch pizza pan
3 tbsp	olive oil
3–4	garlic cloves, cut in thin slivers
1/2 tsp	salt
1/4 tsp	pepper
1 tsp	dried rubbed sage leaves (or 1 tbsp chopped fresh sage)
3 cups	thinly sliced, unpeeled red or white potatoes
2	medium red onions, thinly sliced
1 cup	cheese: crumbled gorgonzola, shredded fontina or shredded mozzarella

1. Allow pizza crust to rest, covered, in warm place for 30 minutes (for slightly thicker crust only) while preparing topping. In large bowl, combine oil, garlic, salt, pepper and sage; add potatoes and onions and toss to coat. Arrange potatoes and onions in overlapping concentric circles on pizza dough. Sprinkle cheese on top.

2. Bake at 450°F on lowest shelf of oven for 20 to 30 minutes or until potatoes are tender, crust is brown and cheese is melted.

pizza rustica

This recipe is a cross between a deep dish pizza and the thick double-crust savory pies that are so popular in Sicily. The ingredients are layered like a torte, then wrapped and sealed in herbed pizza dough. This version is more labor-intensive than a normal pizza, but you'll find it's worth the extra effort to present this impressive dish to a larger group. It's perfect for buffets or picnics because you can make it ahead of time and serve it either hot or at room temperature. To save time, prepare the filling while machine makes the dough.

YIELD: 8 main-course servings

TIPS
*For ease of cutting, cool the pie completely.
If necessary, make the pie a day ahead of time, cool it completely and refrigerate overnight. Before serving, bring it to room temperature or reheat if desired (it will be messier to slice).*

INGREDIENTS

1 recipe	Basic or Herbed Pizza Dough (page 85)
2 tbsp	olive oil
4	large red peppers, sliced in strips
6	cloves garlic, minced
1/4 tsp	pepper
2 tsp	dried oregano (or 2 tbsp chopped fresh oregano)
2 pkgs (10 oz/300g)	frozen chopped spinach, thawed
1 1/2 cups	light ricotta cheese
1/2 cup	grated Parmesan cheese
1/4 tsp	pepper (or dried chili peppers to taste)
1/4 tsp	nutmeg
12 oz	salami, turkey salami or salami with prosciutto or mortadella, thinly sliced
12 oz	provolone, fontina or mozzarella cheese, sliced

VARIATION
Lattice Top Pizza Rustica
Interchange pepper and cheese layers so that you end with peppers. Roll the smaller piece of dough for the top as directed. Cut into 3/4-inch strips and make a lattice top over filling, leaving spaces between the strips so you can see the peppers. Form border with lower crust and ends of strips, crimp edges and bake as directed above.

1. Prepare filling layers while dough is being made. In large skillet heat oil and cook peppers, stirring often, for about 7 minutes or until softened. Add garlic, pepper and oregano, cook 1 to 2 minutes longer, then cool. Squeeze moisture from spinach and mix with ricotta, Parmesan, pepper and nutmeg; set aside. Lightly oil or spray a 9-inch springform pan and coat with cornmeal.
2. Remove dough from machine, cover and let rest for 5 to 10 minutes. Cut dough into 2 pieces, one slightly larger than the other, and cover smaller piece until needed. On lightly floured surface, roll and pat the larger piece of dough to a 15- to 16-inch circle. Fit into prepared pan, pressing along sides and bottom and allowing dough to overhang top edge.
3. Layer half of meat in bottom of pan; spread half of spinach mixture on top, then half of peppers and half of cheese.

(recipe cont'd)

4. Repeat layers ending with cheese. Roll out remaining dough to a 10-inch circle, lay over top of pie and with scissors trim 1 inch beyond pan edge. Press edges of dough together to seal. Roll both layers of crust inwards to form a border, crimping the edges together to seal. (The pie may be refrigerated for up to 2 hours at this point.)

5. Make 2 or 3 slits in top crust to vent. Bake on lowest shelf in 425°F oven for 1 to 1 1/2 hours or until a knife inserted through vent comes out hot. Cool 20 minutes on rack, remove sides of springform pan, and cool at least 20 minutes or longer on rack to allow cheese to set. Cut into wedges to serve warm or at room temperature.

mediterranean stuffed rolls

Stromboli is a cheese bread that was named after a volcanic island off the coast of Sicily because during baking the cheese bubbles up like a volcano. These rolls, which are a miniature version of Stromboli, are great for a walk-about lunch or snack and will give brown-baggers a change of pace.
YIELD: 8 rolls

TIPS
The spinach should be well drained in a sieve but not squeezed dry.

For a slightly thicker crust, shape the rolls, then cover and let rise until they are almost doubled in size (about 45 minutes), then continue as directed above.

For a decorative touch add toppings such as fresh parsley sprigs, long chive sprays, green onion slices, basil leaves or dried herbs, if you like.

DOUGH

1 1/2 cups	water
3 tbsp	olive or vegetable oil
1 tsp	salt
1/2 tsp	pepper
4 cups	white flour*
1 cup	freshly grated Asiago or Parmesan cheese
2 tsp	dried chopped chives or parsley
1 1/2 tsp	bread-machine or instant yeast

FILLING

1 pkg (10 oz/300g) frozen spinach, thawed and well drained (see Tip)	
1 tbsp	vegetable oil
1 cup	shredded mozzarella cheese
1 cup	crumbled feta cheese
1/4–1/2 tsp	pepper or dried chili peppers
1/2 cup	sliced fresh basil leaves (or 2 tsp dried basil)
1 cup	diced, thinly sliced salami, prosciutto or ham

GLAZE

1 egg beaten with 1 tbsp water	

*In Canada use all-purpose or bread flour; in the United States use bread flour.

1. Add dough ingredients to machine according to manufacturer's directions. Select dough cycle. Combine filling ingredients while machine prepares dough. When cycle is complete, remove dough to lightly floured surface; cover and let rest 5 to 10 minutes.
2. Cut into 8 pieces and roll or press each piece into 5- x 6-inch rectangle. Spread 1/2 cup filling over each piece of dough, leaving a 1/4-inch border along one of the long sides. Loosely roll up from long side, jelly-roll style; to seal, pinch edges and pinch ends under.
3. Place rolls seam-side down on lightly greased or parchment-lined baking sheet. Brush with glaze and, if desired, arrange fresh herbs on top or sprinkle with dried herbs. (If you use fresh herbs, brush them with oil.) Make 3 or 4 slits on top with sharp knife.
4. Bake at 375°F for 35 to 40 minutes; cover with foil during last 8 to 10 minutes to prevent fresh herbs from getting too brown.

broccoli and chicken calzone

TIPS

Use thinly sliced deli chicken or leftover roast or grilled chicken in this recipe.
It's easier to roll out dough on a lightly greased counter or baking sheet.

VARIATIONS

Add fresh herbs (such as basil, oregano and fennel), anise seeds or pine nuts to taste.
Substitute 1/2 cup pesto sauce for half of the pizza sauce and substitute fontina or provolone cheese for the mozzarella.
Instead of the diced chicken or turkey, use sliced cooked mushrooms, chopped fennel, canned artichokes, cooked ground beef or turkey, chopped ham or salami.
Substitute grated Parmesan for half of the mozzarella cheese.

Large Calzone
Press dough into 12-inch pizza pan. Spread filling over half of dough, leaving a 1/2-inch border, and sprinkle filling with cheese. Moisten edges with water and fold other half of dough over filling. Pinch and crimp edges to seal. Brush with glaze, sprinkle with Parmesan cheese and bake as directed. Cut into wedges or slices to serve.

Small Snack Calzone
Divide dough into 12 pieces and press into 3-inch squares. Divide filling and cheese evenly among the squares. Close as directed, glaze and bake 15 to 20 minutes.

Tex-Mex Filling
Substitute salsa for the pizza sauce, olives for the hot peppers and Monterey Jack cheese for the mozzarella.

Pizza in a pocket is a good way to describe this favorite Italian on-the-go lunch, supper or snack. I find these bundles easier to make and handle than the traditional half-moon shapes. The larger traditional shape can be sliced and served at the table, and the smaller calzone make great appetizers. Create new combinations according to your own flavor preferences with whatever ingredients you have on hand.

YIELD: 6 calzone

INGREDIENTS	
1	recipe Herbed Pizza Dough (page 85)
FILLING	
1 pkg (10 oz/300g)	frozen chopped broccoli, thawed and drained (or 2 cups finely chopped cooked broccoli)
1 cup	cooked diced chicken or turkey
1 cup	pizza sauce
2	large cloves garlic, minced
1/4 cup	chopped pickled hot banana peppers (optional)
2 cups	shredded mozzarella cheese
GLAZE	
	1 egg beaten with 1 tbsp water

1. When dough cycle is complete, remove dough to lightly floured surface; cover and let rest 5 to 10 minutes. In small bowl combine broccoli, chicken, pizza sauce and garlic.

2. Cut dough into 6 pieces and roll or pat each into 7- x 6-inch rectangle. Place a heaping 1/3 cup of broccoli mixture in the middle of each rectangle and sprinkle cheese evenly on top of filling. Bring 2 opposite corners of dough to the center, pinching points to seal.

Bring 2 remaining corners to center, and pinch all points to seal. Place on lightly greased or parchment-lined baking sheet and brush with glaze.

3. Bake at 425°F for 20 to 25 minutes or until golden brown. (If baking 2 pans at once, use middle and lower racks and reverse positions after 12 minutes.) Cool slightly on racks before serving. If calzone are to be eaten at room temperature, or reheated later, cool completely before wrapping.

sun-dried tomato and garlic focaccia

The name of this earthy Italian flatbread derives from the Latin word focus, meaning hearth, which is where it was originally baked. Focaccia is usually topped with herbed oils, but the sun-dried tomatoes in my version add a wonderful color and flavor. There is also a plainer whole-wheat variation. This flatbread is delicious as an appetizer or with meals in place of garlic bread. Thicker versions can be sliced in half horizontally for sandwiches. To get a more authentic lighter texture, make the focaccia in two stages over two or three days (see Variations).

YIELD: 1 flatbread

DOUGH	
1 1/4 cups	water
2 tbsp	olive oil
3/4 tsp	each salt and sugar
1 tsp	minced garlic
1 tbsp	dried onion flakes
3 cups	white flour*
2 tsp	bread-machine or instant yeast
1/3 cup	chopped sun-dried tomatoes (not oil packed)
TOPPINGS	
2 tbsp	olive oil
1 tbsp	chopped fresh rosemary (or 1 tsp dried)
2 tsp	chopped fresh sage leaves (or 1/2 tsp dried)

*In Canada use all-purpose or bread flour; in the United States use bread flour.

1. Add all dough ingredients except sun-dried tomatoes to machine according to manufacturer's directions. Select dough cycle. Add tomatoes at ingredient signal (or about 20 to 30 minutes into cycle). When cycle is complete, remove dough to lightly floured surface; cover and let rest 5 to 10 minutes.

2. Stretch, push and pat dough into lightly greased 15- x 10-inch shallow baking pan. Cover with clean tea towel and let rise in warm place for 30 minutes or until doubled in height.

3. With handle of wooden spoon or fingers make indentations in dough at 1 1/2-inch intervals to give a dimpled effect. Combine oil and herbs and brush on top.

4. Bake at 450°F on lowest oven shelf for 15 to 20 minutes or until crust is browned. Cut in squares or bars to serve warm.

TIPS
To make a thicker focaccia, roll or pat the dough into a 1/2-inch-thick circle and place on lightly greased or parchment-lined baking sheets. Allow dough to rise, then bake as directed.

For sandwiches, cut thicker round focaccia into wedges, slice in half horizontally and fill with grilled vegetables, meats or cheese.

To reheat, toast focaccia on a rack in the oven until the crust is crisp but not dry.

If you use oil-packed sun-dried tomatoes, drain off the oil, pat the tomatoes dry with paper towel and knead them into the dough by hand before shaping.

VARIATIONS
For a lighter texture, refrigerate sealed dough for 24 to 36 hours; allow dough to warm to room temperature for about 1 1/2 hours, then proceed as directed above.

For whole-wheat focaccia, use equal portions of whole-wheat flour and white flour, and omit the garlic and tomatoes. Brush top with herb- or garlic-flavored oil, as directed above, and bake.

Substitute olives or crisp bacon pieces for the tomatoes.

Vary the herbs to suit your own taste or sprinkle top with coarse sea salt, coarse pepper or grated Parmesan cheese.

sweet fruit focaccia

Sweet focaccia is increasing in popularity and it makes a good alternative to muffins or coffee cake for breakfast, brunch or snacks since it is not as sweet. The contrast between the sweet raisins and the tart cranberries was a winning combination with tasters. The idea for the grape topping was inspired by Schiacciata, a popular Tuscan bread that is made during the wine harvest; according to tradition, the raisins symbolize past harvests and the grapes represent the present harvest. If desired, omit the cranberries when using grapes.

YIELD: 1 large flatbread

DOUGH	
1 1/4 cups	water
2 tbsp	vegetable oil
3/4 tsp	salt
3 tbsp	liquid honey
1 1/2 cups	white flour*
1 1/2 cups	semolina
2 tsp	bread-machine or instant yeast
1/3 cup	each golden raisins and dried cranberries
TOPPINGS (optional)	
1 cup	halved black or red seedless grapes
	melted butter and sugar

*In Canada use all-purpose or bread flour; in the United States use bread flour.

TIPS

This dough will be slightly sticky.

Place a damp cloth under the pan to prevent movement when shaping the dough.

Semolina, a high-gluten white flour milled from the endosperm of durum wheat, is also used in pasta. Fine semolina is called durum flour in some stores.

VARIATION

Substitute figs and walnuts for the raisins and cranberries and top with fresh rosemary sprigs instead of grapes. (Focaccia is often made this way in Italy.)

1. Add all dough ingredients except raisins and cranberries to machine according to manufacturer's directions. Select dough cycle. Add raisins and cranberries at the ingredient signal (or 20 to 30 minutes into cycle). When cycle is complete, remove dough, shape into ball, place in large sealed bag and refrigerate 24 to 36 hours. Remove from refrigerator and let rest at room temperature about 1 1/2 hours.

2. Cut bag away, place dough on lightly floured surface and knead with floured hands 2 or 3 times. Stretch, push and pat the dough into a lightly greased 15- x 10-inch shallow baking pan. (For a thicker bread, press dough into a 12- to 14-inch oval on a baking sheet.) Cover and let rise in warm place for 15 minutes.

3. If desired, lightly press grapes, cut side down, into surface of dough.

4. Bake at 450°F on lowest oven shelf for 15 to 18 minutes. Brush with melted butter or milk and sprinkle with sugar if desired.

leek, mushroom and asiago galette

TIPS
Double the dough recipe and make one of each kind of galette. Place a damp cloth under pizza pan or baking sheet to prevent movement when shaping. To cut basil without bruising, place a number of basil leaves one on top of the other, roll up tightly like a cigar and slice crosswise with sharp knife.

VARIATION
Cheesy Tomato and Basil Galette
Prepare and shape dough as directed above. Toss 2 cups shredded mozzarella cheese with 1/4 cup thinly sliced fresh basil and 3/4 tsp dried rosemary. Sprinkle cheese mixture on rolled out dough, leaving a 2-inch border. Slice about 3 plum tomatoes and arrange on cheese in two concentric circles. Season tomatoes with pepper to taste. Fold border in over filling as directed above. Crumble 3 oz gorgonzola cheese over filling. Beat 1 egg with 1 tbsp water and brush on outside edges of dough and sprinkle with dried basil if desired. Bake as directed above. Garnish center with basil leaves if desired.

Galettes are French, flat, free-form savory or sweet pies. The savory ones are a cross between a pizza and a tart — the crust is more tender than pizza dough and the fillings are usually more substantial than pizza toppings. Served with a salad they make terrific supper or luncheon dishes, and smaller servings make an excellent first course. Since they are equally good at room temperature, take one on a picnic. The Cheesy Tomato and Basil Galette is even faster to make since the filling requires no cooking.

YIELD: 1 12-inch pie

	DOUGH
1/3 cup	water
1	large egg
3 tbsp	margarine or butter
1/2 tsp	salt
1/2 tsp	sugar
3/4 cup	white flour*
3/4 cup	whole-wheat flour
1 tsp	bread-machine or instant yeast
	FILLING
2 tbsp	butter or margarine
4	large leeks, sliced (white and pale green part only)
3 cups	assorted mushrooms, sliced (cremini, portabello, white, oyster or shitake)
3	cloves garlic, minced
3 tbsp	chopped fresh tarragon (or 1 tsp dried)
1/4 tsp	pepper
1/2 cup	dry white wine, chicken broth or water
1	egg, beaten and divided
1/2 cup	cream (10% or 18%)
2 cups	freshly shredded Asiago or grated Parmesan cheese
1/4 cup	chopped parsley (optional)

*In Canada use all-purpose or bread flour; in the United States use bread flour.

1. Add all dough ingredients to machine according to manufacturer's directions. Select dough cycle.
2. Prepare filling while machine makes dough. Heat butter in large skillet over medium heat. Add leeks, mushrooms, garlic, tarragon and pepper and cook, stirring often, for 5 to 7 minutes. Add wine and cook until all liquid has evaporated. Set aside 1 tbsp of beaten egg and mix remaining egg into cream. Stir cream into leek mixture with 1 1/2 cups cheese and set aside to cool.
3. When cycle is complete, remove dough to lightly floured surface; cover and let rest 5 to 10 minutes.

4. Roll or press dough into 12-inch circle on lightly greased baking sheet or pizza pan. Spread filling on dough leaving 1-inch border around the outer edges. Fold border in over filling, pleating or overlapping as necessary. Brush reserved beaten egg on outer edges of dough and sprinkle with dried tarragon if desired. Sprinkle remaining cheese in the center over filling.
5. Bake at 400°F on bottom shelf of oven for 20 to 25 minutes. Cool 10 minutes. Garnish center with parsley if desired and cut into wedges to serve warm or at room temperature.

fougasse

This sculpted leaf-shaped bread, also known as fouace, was traditionally the centerpiece and one of the thirteen desserts served at Christmas celebrations in Provence. Today it is baked year-round and the savory version is often scented with herbs or studded with bacon, anchovies or olives; my husband Allan and I enjoyed one made with Roquefort cheese while sitting on the shore of the Riviera. Start this recipe two to three days before you want to serve it. It is best eaten warm, broken at the table, and it goes well with soft cheeses or salads.

YIELD: 1 flatbread.

DOUGH	
1 1/4 cups	water
2 tbsp	olive oil
3/4 tsp	salt
3 cups	white flour*
2 tsp	bread-machine or instant yeast
TOPPING	
2 tbsp	olive oil
1 tsp	Herbes de Provence or other herb blend (see Tips)
	olive slices or anchovy pieces (optional)

*In Canada use all-purpose or bread flour; in the United States use bread flour.

TIPS

Place a damp cloth under the baking sheet to prevent movement when shaping.

For a crispier crust, spray dough or oven walls with water, two to three times during baking.

Herbes de Provence is a dried herb blend that is commonly used in southern France for seasoning meats and vegetables. It usually contains basil, rosemary, sage, marjoram, summer savory, thyme, fennel seeds and lavender. Look for it in specialty food stores or in the gourmet or spice sections of supermarkets, or create your own blend.

1. Add all dough ingredients to machine according to manufacturer's directions. Select dough cycle. When cycle is complete, remove dough, shape into a ball, place in large sealed bag and refrigerate for 24 to 36 hours. Remove dough from refrigerator and let rest at room temperature about 1 1/2 hours.

2. When ready to bake, cut away bag and place dough on lightly greased baking sheet and press with palm of hand to flatten. Stretch and pat dough into an oval, teardrop or triangular shape about 1/2-inch thick with 10-inch base. With sharp knife or razor make 3-inch diagonal slashes, about 2 inches apart down each side of shape (to give effect of veins in a leaf) and use fingers to widen slashes 2 to 3 times original size so they won't close when baked. Mix 1 tbsp oil with herbs, brush on top and decorate with olives or anchovies if desired. Let rest 15 minutes.

3. Bake at 450°F on bottom oven shelf for 18 to 22 minutes or until golden brown and crisp on bottom. Remove from oven and immediately brush with remaining 1 tbsp oil. Cool slightly on rack; serve warm.

chapter six

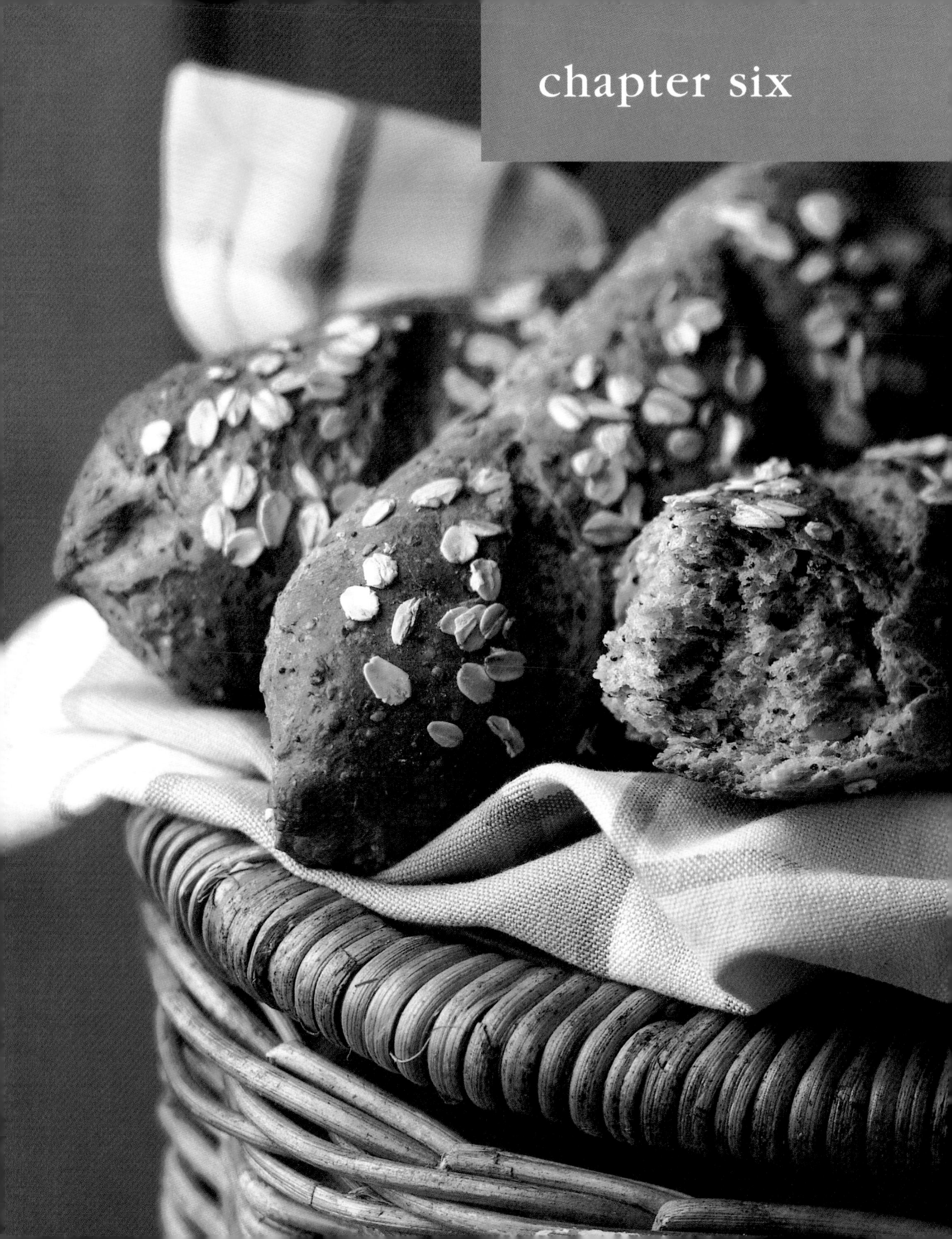

This chapter presents a varied collection of buns, breads, breadsticks and bagels that can be shaped from dough made in the bread machine. Buns are one of the most versatile small breads. They hold hamburgers, hot dogs or sandwich fillings. There are soft, rich dinner or breakfast rolls in a variety of shapes (for example, Cheddar Wheat Rolls or Sicilian Breakfast Twists). There are also large crusty buns (made from Ciabatta dough as well as from Sourdough or French Bread dough in chapter 1). The Herbed Cheese and Onion Twists and the Lemon and Parsley Spiral Rolls are slightly more time-consuming but worth the effort. There are also yummy sweet buns, such as Orange Caramel Sticky Buns, Chelsea Buns and Cinnamon Buns as well as the traditional Hot Cross Buns (see chapter 7). Pretzels, breadsticks and bagels are small breads eaten in hand for snacks, for breakfast or with meals. Finally, you can expand your repertoire of artisan loaves with Nutty Seed Baguettes, Healthy Flaxseed Peasant Bread and Swiss Cheese and Mushroom Loaf.

cheddar wheat rolls

onion mustard baked pretzels

herbed cheese and onion twists

lemon and parsley spiral rolls

oat and flax bagels

swiss cheese and mushroom loaf

ciabatta

nutty seed and oatmeal baguette

healthy flaxseed peasant bread

orange caramel sticky buns

sicilian breakfast twists

cheddar wheat rolls

These light, flavorful rolls will impress your guests. Try out different shapes and toppings each time you make them. Our favorite hamburger bun is also made with this dough and topped with cheese and sliced onions (see Variations). My assistant Bev Watson likes to add cubes of cheese to the dough to create pockets of melted cheese in the rolls.

TIP
Omit shredded cheese. Chill 1 1/4 to 1 1/2 cups cubed cheese in freezer for 15 minutes and add at the ingredient signal (or about 20 to 30 minutes into cycle).

VARIATIONS
Clover Leaf Rolls
Grease 12 (for large batch) or 18 (for extra-large batch) muffin tins. Cut dough into 12 or 18 pieces and divide each piece in three. Shape small pieces into smooth balls, and place 3 balls in each muffin cup. Cover and let rise in warm place for about 30 minutes or until doubled in size. Bake at 375°F for 10 to 12 minutes or until golden brown. For a soft crust, brush with softened or melted butter.

Hamburger or Hot Dog Buns
Cut dough into 9 (for large batch) or 12 (for extra-large batch) pieces. Shape into smooth balls for hamburger buns or ropes for hot dog buns. Place on greased baking sheet 3 inches apart, and flatten slightly for hamburger buns or flatten to 1/2-inch thickness for hot dog buns. Cover, let rise, then brush with egg and add toppings if desired. Bake at 375°F for 12 to 15 minutes or until crust is golden brown.

12 ROLLS	DOUGH	16 ROLLS
1 1/4 cups	water	1 1/2 cups
2 tbsp	margarine or butter	3 tbsp
3/4 tsp	salt	1 tsp
2 tbsp	brown sugar, packed	3 tbsp
1 tbsp	instant skim-milk powder	2 tbsp
1 1/2 cups	white flour*	2 cups
1 1/2 cups	whole-wheat flour	2 cups
1/4 tsp	powdered mustard	1/2 tsp
1/4 tsp	dried, rubbed sage leaves (optional)	1/2 tsp
1 1/4 tsp	bread-machine or instant yeast	1 1/2 tsp
1 1/4 cups	coarsely shredded old Cheddar cheese	1 1/2 cups
	GLAZE	
	1 egg beaten with 1 tbsp water or milk	
	TOPPINGS (optional)	
	shredded Cheddar cheese, thinly sliced onion, dried dill, thyme, rosemary or sage, poppy or sesame seeds	

*In Canada use all-purpose or bread flour; in the United States use bread flour.

1. Add all ingredients for dough to machine according to manufacturer's directions. Select dough cycle. When cycle is complete, remove dough to lightly floured surface; cover and let rest 5 to 10 minutes.

2. Cut dough into 12 or 16 pieces; shape each into a smooth ball and place in greased muffin tins. Cover with clean tea towel and let rise in warm place for about 30 minutes or until doubled in size. Brush with glaze and, if desired, sprinkle with your choice of toppings.

3. Bake at 375°F for 10 to 12 minutes or until golden brown. Remove rolls from pans and serve warm or leave to cool on racks.

onion mustard baked pretzels

TIPS

If baking 2 pans at once, reverse positions and rotate halfway through baking time. For a softer pretzel, after shaping, cover and let rise in a warm place for 20 to 30 minutes, then glaze, add toppings and bake as directed.

The history of pretzels can be traced all the way back to the Roman Empire. In Germany pretzels are a popular snack with beer, and in New York hot pretzels are topped with mustard. In this version I have incorporated the mustard into the dough. The twisted knot shape takes longer to form so if you are in a hurry, make pretzel sticks; vary the size depending on whether the pretzels are to be served with drinks, with soups or as snacks.

YIELD: 8 or 12 pretzels

VARIATION
Pretzel Sticks
Divide dough into 12 pieces, roll each piece into 6- to 7-inch log and place a few inches apart on prepared baking sheet. With sharp knife make 3 to 4 diagonal slashes across the top. Brush with glaze and sprinkle with toppings. Bake at 400°F for 20 to 25 minutes.

DOUGH	
1 1/4 cups	water
1 tbsp	vegetable oil
3/4 tsp	salt
1 tbsp	sugar
3 tbsp	prepared mustard
3 cups	white flour*
3 tbsp	dried onion flakes
1 1/2 tsp	bread-machine or instant yeast
GLAZE	
1 egg beaten with 1 tbsp water	
TOPPINGS	
poppy seeds, sesame seeds or coarse salt	

*In Canada use all-purpose or bread flour; in the United States use bread flour.

1. Add all dough ingredients to machine according to manufacturer's directions. Select dough cycle. When cycle is complete, remove dough to lightly floured surface; cover and let rest 5 to 10 minutes.
2. Cut into 8 to 12 pieces (depending on size desired) and roll each piece into a 16-inch rope. Pick up ends of one rope and form into a horseshoe on lightly greased or parchment-lined baking sheets; cross ends and twist once and bring ends up to top of horseshoe and press down lightly. Repeat with remaining ropes, leaving a 1-inch space between each pretzel. Brush with glaze and sprinkle with salt or seeds.
3. Bake at 400°F for 15 to 18 minutes or until golden brown.

herbed cheese and onion twists

Start with savory herbed dough wrapped around golden onions and, if desired, add cheese to make French Onion Twists.

YIELD: 20 rolls

DOUGH

1 1/3 cups	water
1 tbsp	olive or vegetable oil
3/4 tsp	salt
1 tsp	sugar
3 cups	white flour*
1/4 cup	grated Parmesan cheese
3/4 tsp	each dried basil and oregano
1/2 tsp	each dried marjoram and garlic powder
1 1/4 tsp	bread-machine or instant yeast

FILLING

2 cups	finely chopped onion
2 tbsp	butter, margarine or olive oil

GLAZE

1 egg beaten with 1 tbsp water

TOPPINGS (optional)

coarse sea salt or sesame, poppy, fennel or celery seeds

*In Canada use all-purpose or bread flour; in the United States use bread flour.

VARIATIONS

French Onion Twists

Roll out dough and spread with onions as directed; sprinkle 1 cup shredded Swiss or Cheddar cheese on top of onions and continue as directed.

Herbed Bread Sticks

Yield: *24*

Prepare dough as directed. Divide into 4 pieces and roll into 12- x 6-inch rectangles. Cut rectangles into 6 strips and place a few inches apart on lightly greased or parchment-lined baking sheets. Cover and let rise for 20 minutes. Bake at 400°F for 12 to 18 minutes or until golden brown. For crisper sticks, spray with water 2 or 3 times during baking.

To make thicker breadsticks divide dough into 2 pieces. Continue as directed but bake a few minutes longer.

1. Add all dough ingredients to machine according to manufacturer's directions. Select dough cycle.
2. Heat butter in large skillet over medium heat, add onions and cook until golden brown, stirring often; let cool.
3. When cycle is complete, remove dough to lightly floured surface; cover and let rest 5 to10 minutes.

4. Roll dough into 20- x 12-inch rectangle. Spread onions lengthwise over half the dough, leaving 1/2-inch border along the long side; lightly press onions into dough. Fold dough lengthwise over onions to form a 20- x 6-inch rectangle, pressing down lightly and pinching edge to seal. Cut into 20 strips. Twist each strip twice and place on lightly

greased or parchment-lined baking sheet, pressing both ends down.
5. Cover and let rise in a warm place for 20 to 25 minutes. Brush with glaze and sprinkle with salt or seeds if desired.
6. Bake at 400°F for 12 to 15 minutes or until golden.

lemon and parsley spiral rolls

These spirals are similar to the traditional fan rolls, but they are faster to make. The lemon-flavored filling is like gremolata — a mixture of parsley, lemon and garlic that traditionally tops the Italian veal dish osso buco.

YIELD: 18 rolls

DOUGH	
1/2 cup	water
3/4 cup	low-fat sour cream
1	egg
3/4 tsp	salt
3 cups	white flour*
1 tbsp	sugar
1 1/4 tsp	bread-machine or instant yeast
FILLING	
2	lemons, grated zest only
4	cloves garlic, minced
2/3 cup	minced fresh parsley
1 tsp	dried thyme (optional)
2 tbsp	olive oil
GLAZE	
1 egg white beaten with 1 tbsp water	

*In Canada use all-purpose or bread flour; in the United States use bread flour.

TIP

Use dental floss or thread to cut dough: slide floss underneath dough, bring ends up and around where the cut is to be made and cross over at top; to cut dough pull the ends quickly.

If baking two pans at once, place them on the middle and lower oven shelves; reverse positions and rotate halfway through baking.

VARIATIONS
Cheesy Garlic Filling
To make filling, combine 1/2 cup minced parsley, 1/2 cup grated Parmesan cheese, 1/4 cup sesame seeds, 1 tsp dried oregano, 1/2 tsp garlic and 1/2 tsp onion powder. Substitute 3 tbsp softened butter or margarine for the olive oil. Shape buns, let rise and bake as directed.

1. Add all dough ingredients to machine according to manufacturer's directions. Select dough cycle.
2. Combine all filling ingredients except oil. When cycle is complete, remove dough to lightly floured surface; cover and let rest 5 to 10 minutes.
3. Cut dough into 2 equal pieces and roll each into a 13 1/2- x 10-inch rectangle. Brush each rectangle with 1 tbsp oil and sprinkle evenly with half the filling, leaving 1/2-inch border along the long edge. Press filling into dough lightly with hands. From long side roll rectangles up jelly-roll style and pinch edges to seal; cut each roll into 9 1-1/2-inch pieces (see Tips). Place pieces, seams down, on lightly greased or parchment-lined baking sheet and let rest 5 minutes. Press the handle of a wooden spoon firmly down on the center of each roll almost to the bottom making a deep crease and causing cut ends to fan out.
4. Cover and let rise in warm place about 30 minutes or until almost doubled in bulk.
5. Brush with glaze and bake at 375°F for 12 to 15 minutes or until golden brown.

oat and flax bagels

The earliest historical documentations of bagels date back to the 17th century. The name comes from the Yiddish word beygl, meaning ring. Bagels are fun to make but they do require some work so I like to make a healthy grain variety that you can't always buy in the stores. Vary the method to get the texture you prefer; your bagels may not be the same as Montreal, New York or Toronto bagels but they'll be delicious just the same!

YIELD: 10 or 12 bagels

DOUGH	
1 1/4 cups	water
1 tsp	salt
3 tbsp	honey
1 1/2 cups	white flour*
1 cup	whole wheat flour
1 cup	rolled oats
3/4 cup	ground flaxseed (see Tips)
1 1/2 tsp	bread-machine or instant yeast

GLAZE (optional)
1 egg beaten with 1 tbsp water

TOPPINGS (optional)
flaxseed, sesame seeds, poppy seeds, rolled oats or a mixture

*In Canada use all-purpose or bread flour; in the United States use bread flour.

1. Add all dough ingredients to machine according to manufacturer's directions. Select dough cycle. When cycle is complete, remove dough to lightly floured surface; cover and let rest 5 to 10 minutes.
2. Cut into 10 or 12 pieces and cover with tea towel.

3. Shape 3 pieces at a time into smooth balls by pulling dough down, under, pinching together at bottom. To form rings, place balls on the counter and press thumb and index finger into center, making a hole in the middle; expand hole with floured fingers until it is about 2 to 2 1/2 inches in diameter. Continue rolling the ring with

floured hands to make a smooth circle. Repeat with each piece of dough.

4. For a dense, chewy texture, boil the rings immediately (see step 5). For a more tender texture, cover rings and let rise in a warm place for 20 to 30 minutes before boiling. For convenience, refrigerate the dough for 4 to 24 hours, then shape and boil.

5. Combine 12 cups water and 2 tbsp honey or sugar in a large saucepan. Bring to boil and reduce heat to medium. Drop 2 or 3 bagels into water at a time (don't over-crowd), cook 1 minute, turn and cook 1 minute longer. With a slotted spoon remove from water and place on wire rack over a pan or towel to drain a few seconds. If desired, dip one or both sides into toppings of your choice.

6. Place bagels on lightly greased or parchment-lined baking sheet. If no toppings are applied, brush with glaze to give a shiny top.

7. Bake at 425°F for 10 minutes, turn and bake an additional 10 to 15 minutes (depending on size) until bagels sound hollow when tapped on bottom. Transfer to a rack to cool.

swiss cheese and mushroom loaf

VARIATION
Finger Rolls
Divide dough into 12 pieces and shape into ovals. Arrange 6 ovals on lightly greased or parchment-lined baking sheet in a row just touching one another; repeat with remaining 6 pieces. Cover and let rise as directed, and bake for 15 to 20 minutes.

The rich golden texture of this loaf is marbled with flecks of mushrooms. Each variety of mushroom has its own distinct flavor; cultivated mushrooms are milder while woodland or field mushrooms such as porcini or cepes have a stronger flavor. The Swiss cheese also adds a nutty taste. For a buffet table, shape this dough into finger rolls (see Variation) so guests can pull off separate rolls.

YIELD: 1 loaf or 12 rolls

INGREDIENTS

2/3 cup	water
1 tbsp	margarine or butter
3	large eggs
3/4 tsp	salt
1/4 tsp	ground nutmeg or pepper
3 cups	white flour*
1/3 cup	dried mushroom pieces
2 cups	shredded Swiss cheese, divided
1 1/4 tsp	bread-machine or instant yeast

*In Canada use all-purpose or bread flour; in the United States use bread flour.

1. Set aside 2/3 cup of cheese; add all remaining ingredients to machine according to manufacturer's directions. Select dough cycle. When cycle is complete, remove dough to lightly floured surface; cover and let rest 5 to 10 minutes.

2. Divide dough into 6 pieces and shape each piece into an oval. On a lightly greased baking sheet arrange ovals in a row just touching one another. Cover and let rise in warm place for 20 to 30 minutes or until doubled in bulk.

3. Sprinkle reserved cheese on top. Bake at 400°F for 20 to 25 minutes or until crust is golden brown and an instant-read thermometer inserted in center reads 200°F. Cool on rack.

ciabatta

Ciabatta is an Italian word meaning slipper, and the shape of this loaf indeed resembles a well-worn slipper. This recipe uses the sponge method to create a unique, airy texture and flavor (see Tip). Sandwiches made from ciabatta bread or buns have become quite popular on restaurant menus. Drizzle slices or halved buns with olive oil and fill with grilled vegetables, prosciutto and fresh basil, or grilled chicken and arugula.

YIELD: 2 loaves or 8 buns

SPONGE

2/3 cup	warm water
1/4 tsp	sugar
1 cup	white flour*
1/2 tsp	active dry, bread-machine or instant yeast

DOUGH

3/4 cup	water
1 tbsp	olive oil
1 1/2 tsp	salt
2 cups	white flour*
1/2 tsp	active dry, bread-machine or instant yeast

*In Canada use all-purpose or bread flour; in the United States use bread flour.

1. Add the sponge ingredients to machine according to manufacturer's directions. Select dough cycle. Allow to mix for 5 to 10 minutes, scraping down sides of pan with rubber spatula as needed. Shut machine off and leave sponge to develop in machine for 12 or up to 24 hours.

2. Add remaining dough ingredients according to manufacturer's directions. Select dough cycle. Scrape down sides of pan with rubber spatula during first mixing. If possible stop the machine a few minutes before the cycle ends. (Some cycles end with a final kneading that would deflate air bubbles.)

3. When cycle is finished, remove dough with well-floured hands. Divide dough in half and place each half on well-floured or parchment-lined baking sheet. Pull and stretch dough into a rough oval shape (about 12 x 4 inches), rounding and tucking under the edges. Dust generously with flour and allow to rise uncovered in a warm place for about 20 minutes.

4. Bake at 425°F for about 30 minutes or until crust is golden brown (or an instant-read thermometer inserted in the center reads 200°F). Cool on wire rack.

TIP

A sponge is a wet yeast mixture that needs to be made one or two days before the loaf is baked. When shaping the dough, handle it very gently so the air bubbles don't break and resist the temptation to add more flour.

This dough will be wet and sticky and will not form a ball.

For a crispier crust, spray the loaves with cold water 2 or 3 times during baking.

If baking two loaves at once, place on lower and middle racks and reverse and rotate baking sheets about halfway through baking time.

VARIATION

Ciabatta Buns

Prepare dough as directed above. Divide dough into 8 pieces and shape into smooth balls by pulling dough down and under. Dip smooth top into flour and place, floured side up, on floured or parchment-lined baking sheet. Allow to rise covered, about 45 to 60 minutes or until not quite doubled in bulk. Bake at 425°F for 25 minutes (spraying with water if desired) or until buns sound hollow when tapped underneath (or an instant-read thermometer inserted in center reads 200°F).

nutty seed and oatmeal baguette

Baguette is a French word meaning stick — an apt name for the long, narrow loaves of bread that the French also call baguettes. This version is healthier than most of the baguettes you see in the stores. The Épi variation of this loaf is shaped like a stalk of wheat. It is easier to make than it looks, and is fun to serve since the sections can be broken off as individual buns. (Épi is a French word for the ear of corn.)

YIELD: 2 baguettes

TIP

Vary the seeds as desired. You might substitute caraway seeds for the poppy seeds and omit the thyme.

VARIATIONS
Épi
Shape dough into 2 long baguettes as directed. With sharp scissors, make diagonal cuts three-quarters of the way through each loaf at 2-inch intervals. Place on prepared baking sheets. Lift up the first section and twist it to the right (with cut side up), pinching ends to form a point; lift and twist the next section to the left, again pinching ends to form a point. Repeat with remaining sections to create a shape resembling a wheat stalk. Bake as directed. Handle the loaf carefully after baking as the sections can easily break off.

INGREDIENTS

1 1/4 cups	water
3 tbsp	vegetable oil
3/4 tsp	salt
3 tbsp	liquid honey
1 1/2 cups	white flour*
1 cup	whole-wheat flour
3/4 cup	quick-cooking rolled oats
1/4 cup	chopped pecans or California walnuts
2 tbsp	each millet, unsalted sunflower seeds, sesame seeds, poppy seeds and flaxseed
2 tsp	dried thyme (optional)
1 1/4 tsp	bread-machine or instant yeast

*In Canada use all-purpose or bread flour; in the United States use bread flour.

1. Add all ingredients to machine according to manufacturer's directions. Select dough cycle. When cycle is complete, remove dough to lightly floured surface; cover and let rest 5 to 10 minutes.
2. Divide dough into 2 pieces. Cover one; press the other into a small rectangle and roll it up lengthwise tightly, into a log. Roll log back and forth to elongate into a 12- or 15-inch baguette with tapered ends. Place baguette on lightly greased or parchment-lined baking sheet, then repeat with second piece of dough. Cover baguettes with tea towel and let rise in warm place for 35 to 45 minutes.
3. Brush with milk and sprinkle with rolled oats if desired. With sharp, serrated knife make diagonal slashes across the top of loaf.
4. Bake in 400°F oven for 20 to 25 minutes or until golden brown or an instant-read thermo-meter inserted in the center reads 200°F.

healthy flaxseed peasant bread

This relatively heavy, dense bread makes a hearty lunch with a bowl of soup or a fast lunch with a wedge of cheese and an apple. One taster also enjoyed it toasted for breakfast with honey.

YIELD: 1 round loaf

TIPS

Although flaxseed has been receiving much acclaim in recent years, it has been around since the beginning of civilization. It was brought to North America from France in the 17th century. Flaxseed tastes good and it also provides essential nutrients, fatty acids and fiber. We often add whole seeds to baked goods for their texture and nutty flavor but since recent discoveries have shown that the body digests ground or milled flaxseed better, in this recipe I have replaced part of the flour with ground flaxseed. Look for ground flaxseed in the refrigerated section of health stores or grind flaxseed in a coffee or spice grinder as needed.

To maintain its freshness, store milled flaxseed in an airtight, opaque container in the refrigerator up to 30 days.

INGREDIENTS

1 1/2 cups	water
2 tbsp	canola or vegetable oil
1 tsp	salt
3 tbsp	honey
3 tbsp	instant skim-milk powder
1 1/2 cups	white flour*
1 1/4 cups	whole-wheat flour
3/4 cup	oat bran
3/4 cup	natural baking bran
3/4 cup	ground or milled flaxseed
1 1/2 tsp	bread-machine or instant yeast

*In Canada use all-purpose or bread flour; in the United States use bread flour.

1. Add all ingredients to machine according to manufacturer's directions. Select dough cycle. When cycle is complete, remove dough to lightly floured surface; cover and let rest 5 to 10 minutes.

2. Shape dough into smooth ball and press into a 7-inch round. Place in lightly greased 8- or 9-inch round cake pan or pie plate, cover with tea towel and let rise in a warm place for 35 to 45 minutes or until almost doubled in size.

3. With a sharp knife, score the surface of the dough into 8 wedges. Bake at 375°F for 35 to 40 minutes; bread is done when an instant-read thermometer inserted in center reads 200°F. Cool slightly on rack and cut into wedges to serve.

orange caramel sticky buns

This recipe adds a new flavor dimension to the ever-popular gooey sticky buns. The inspiration to add orange came from a sticky bun I tasted in San Antonio, Texas. With slight variations to the ingredients you can use this dough to make the more traditional cinnamon buns or Chelsea buns.

YIELD: 12 buns

DOUGH	
1/2 cup	low-fat milk
1	large egg
3 tbsp	margarine or butter
1/2 tsp	salt
1/4 cup	sugar
2 cups	white flour*
1/2 tsp	ground cinnamon
1 tsp	grated orange rind
1 1/2 tsp	bread-machine or instant yeast
TOPPING	
1/4 cup	corn syrup
1/4 cup	orange juice
1 tsp	grated orange rind
1 tbsp	butter or margarine
1/2 cup	brown sugar, packed
1/3 cup	broken pecan pieces
FILLING	
2 tbsp	butter or margarine, softened
1/3 cup	brown sugar, packed

*In Canada use all-purpose or bread flour; in the United States use bread flour.

TIPS

To bake buns quickly for breakfast or brunch make the dough with 2 tsp yeast. Shape dough, place in pan as directed, cover loosely with plastic wrap and refrigerate for 2 to 24 hours. Let stand at room temperature or in a warm place for 15 to 20 minutes, then bake as directed.

You can also wrap and freeze unbaked, unrisen rolls in the pan for up to three months. After defrosting, allow buns to rise, then bake as directed.

Use dental floss or thread to cut dough: slide floss underneath dough, bring ends up and around where the cut is to be made and cross over at top; pull the ends quickly.

(recipe cont'd)

VARIATIONS
Cinnamon Buns
Yield: *12 buns*

Omit topping, and omit cinnamon and orange. Prepare and roll dough as directed above and spread with 3 tbsp soft margarine or butter. For filling, combine 1/4 cup brown sugar, 2 tsp ground cinnamon, 1 tbsp grated lemon rind and 3/4 cup raisins. Sprinkle over dough leaving a 1/2-inch border along one of long sides. Roll up and slice as directed above. Place pieces cut side down in greased muffin pans. Cover and let rise in a warm place about 40 minutes or until doubled in size. Bake at 375°F for 15 to 18 minutes or until browned. Cool 5 to 8 minutes. Using a knife, loosen buns around edges and remove. If desired, drizzle with frosting made by mixing 1/2 cup sifted confectioners' sugar with 2 to 3 tsp milk.

Chelsea Buns
Yield: *9 buns*

In the dough, if desired, substitute lemon rind for the orange rind and ground allspice or nutmeg for the cinnamon. In the topping, substitute 2 tbsp water for the orange juice and omit the orange rind and substitute 9 walnut, pecan or cherry halves for the pecan pieces. In the filling, add 1/2 cup currants or raisins. Prepare dough and topping as directed. Pour topping mixture into greased 8-inch square pan, place the 9 halved nuts or cherries in three rows in the mixture and set aside. Roll out dough, spread with butter or margarine, and sprinkle first with brown sugar, then with raisins or currants. Roll up along short side and cut into 9 slices. Place slices cut side up in prepared pan, on top of nuts or cherries. Rise and bake as directed. Invert pan of buns over serving plate and cool upside down for 5 to 10 minutes before removing pan.

1. Add all dough ingredients to machine according to manufacturer's directions. Select dough cycle.

2. Prepare topping while machine makes dough. In small saucepan combine corn syrup, orange juice, rind, butter and brown sugar. Bring to full rolling boil, stirring constantly, then remove from heat and pour into greased 9-inch round cake pan. Top with pecans and set aside.

3. When cycle is complete, remove dough to lightly floured surface; cover and let rest 5 to 10 minutes.

4. Roll dough into 9- x 12-inch rectangle, spread with 2 tbsp softened butter and sprinkle with brown sugar. From the long side tightly roll up, jelly-roll style, pinching edges to seal. Cut roll into 12 pieces (see Tip). Place 9 slices (cut side down) around the outside of pan and 3 slices in the middle. Cover and let rise in a warm place for 35 to 45 minutes or until doubled in size.

5. Bake at 375°F for 30 to 35 minutes or an instant-read thermometer inserted in center reads 200°F. (Covering buns with foil for the last few minutes will prevent over-browning.) Invert pan of buns over serving plate, allow to cool slightly then remove pan.

sicilian breakfast twists

This recipe was inspired by rolls I ate recently while enjoying the view of Naxos bay and Mount Etna in Taormina, Sicily. These rolls were part of the home-cooked Sicilian breakfast buffet at our small hotel. For a simple but special weekend breakfast, add a little orange marmalade to a fresh fruit salad and serve it with these rolls.

VARIATION

Add 1/3 to 1/2 cup toasted pine nuts at the ingredient signal (or about 20 to 30 minutes into cycle). To toast pine nuts, place in non-stick skillet and cook over medium heat, shaking or stirring until lightly browned.

12 ROLLS	DOUGH	16 ROLLS
3/4 cup	water	1 cup
3 tbsp	margarine or butter	1/4 cup
1	large egg(s)	2
3/4 tsp	salt	1 tsp
1 1/2 tsp	grated orange rind	2 tsp
1/3 cup	sugar	1/2 cup
3 tbsp	instant skim-milk powder	1/4 cup
3 cups	white flour*	4 cups
1/3 cup	dried currants	1/2 cup
1 1/4 tsp	bread-machine or instant yeast	1 1/2 tsp
	GLAZE	
	1 egg yolk beaten with 1 tbsp milk	
	TOPPING	
	confectioners' sugar	

*In Canada use all-purpose or bread flour; in the United States use bread flour.

1. Add all ingredients to machine according to manufacturer's directions. Select dough cycle. When cycle is complete, remove dough to lightly floured surface; cover and let rest 5 to 10 minutes.
2. Divide dough into 12 or 16 pieces and roll each piece into a 14-inch rope. Fold each rope in half and place on lightly greased or parchment-lined baking sheet; twist strands once or twice, pinch ends to seal, and place about 2 inches apart. Cover and let rise in a warm place for 20 to 30 minutes or until doubled in bulk.
3. Brush twists with glaze. Bake in 400°F oven for 15 to 20 minutes or until golden brown. Cool slightly on rack, then lightly sift confectioners' sugar on top. Serve warm or cool completely and seal to freeze.

chapter seven

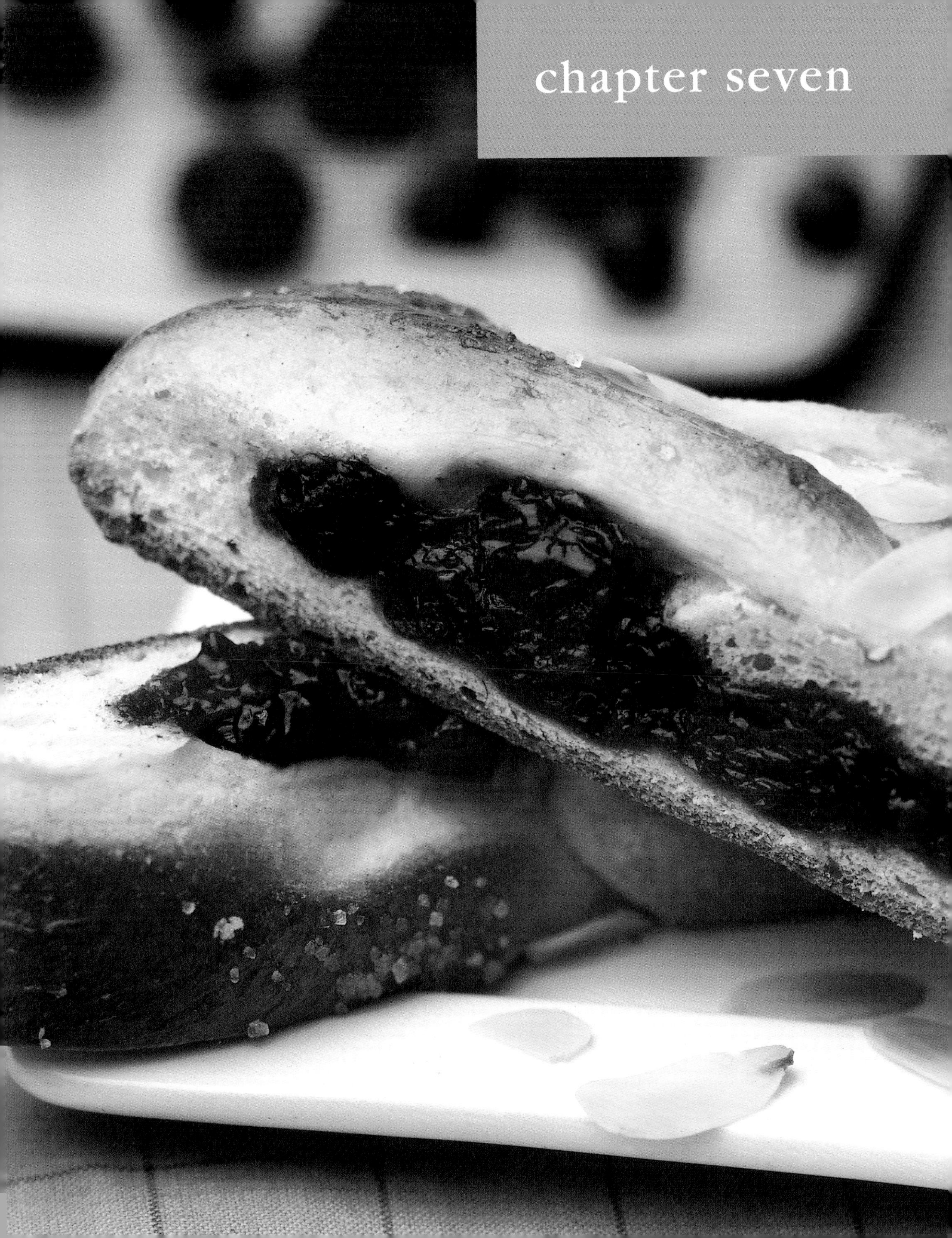

The breads and coffee cakes in this chapter are hand shaped from dough made in the bread machine. Some were inspired by my travels. Others are variations of breads I grew up with, such as the Scandinavian Coffee Cake or the Christstollen that Mom made. Still others, such as Challah, European Pumpernickel and the various Easter and Christmas loaves are versions of breads that I have enjoyed with friends and neighbors.

I am sure that the aromas and flavors of these breads and coffeecakes will remind you of your own family's baking — food customs are one of our strongest connections with our ancestral roots.

Whether you make these loaves to share with family or guests in your home or to give them away as holiday or hostess gifts, I am sure you will discover the pleasure of creating these handcrafted breads and coffee cakes.

challah bread

pane di semola

ham, onion and walnut kugelhopf

pane alle oliva

european pumpernickel bread

hazelnut and poppy-seed
    coffee cake

scandinavian coffee cake

mardis gras coffee cake

bumbleberry coffee cake

greek easter ring and other
    easter breads

christstollen and other
    christmas breads

challah bread

Challah is a braided egg bread, enjoyed for sandwiches and toast because of its wonderful sunny color and rich flavor. This double-braided loaf makes a higher-than-usual loaf, good for sandwiches.

YIELD: 1 loaf

TIP
Use the egg white left over from the dough for the glaze.
If time is short, bake this dough in the bread machine

VARIATIONS
Single Braid
Divide dough into 3 pieces and braid as directed above.

Quick 'n' Easy Lemon Poppy Seed Challah
Add 3 tbsp each poppy seeds and grated lemon rind with flour. Bake bread in bread machine on basic or sweet cycle.

Sweeter Challah
Add 2 tbsp sugar with flour, increase the yeast to 1 1/2 tsp and add 1/2 cup golden raisins at ingredient signal (or about 20 to 30 minutes into cycle).

DOUGH

1/4 cup	water
3 tbsp	margarine or butter
3	eggs plus 1 yolk
3/4 tsp	salt
3 tbsp	honey
3 tbsp	instant skim-milk powder
3 cups	white flour*
pinch	powdered saffron or turmeric (optional)
1 1/4 tsp	bread machine or instant yeast

GLAZE

1 egg white beaten with 1 tbsp water

TOPPING

sesame seeds or poppy seeds

*In Canada use all-purpose or bread flour; in the United States use bread flour.

1. Add all dough ingredients to machine according to manufacturer's directions. Select dough cycle. When cycle is complete, remove dough to lightly floured surface; cover and let rest 5 to 10 minutes.
2. Roll dough into a 9-inch log and cut off one third. Divide the larger portion into 3 pieces and roll each piece into a 15-inch rope. Place ropes on lightly greased or parchment-lined baking sheet.

3. To braid: bring left rope under center rope and lay down; bring right rope under new center rope and lay down; repeat to end. Pinch ends together to seal and tuck under braid. Make a second braid with smaller piece of dough, rolling ropes to 12 inches and place it on top of the first. Cover, let rise in warm place about 40 to 45 minutes or until doubled in bulk.

4. Brush glaze on braid and sprinkle with seeds.
5. Bake at 375°F for 30 to 35 minutes or until crust is golden brown (or an instant-read thermometer inserted in center reads 200°F). (Cover loaf with foil for the last few minutes if necessary to prevent over-browning.) Cool on rack.

pane di semola

VARIATION
Quick 'n' Easy Pane di Semola
*Add all ingredients to machine
according to manufacturer's
directions. Select French or basic
white bread cycle.*

We have enjoyed this traditional bread from southern Italy many times; it is wonderful dipped in olive oil or a mixture of olive oil and balsamic vinegar or grilled to make bruschetta. Semolina (a special grind of durum wheat) is also used in pasta and it gives this bread a nutty taste, a golden color and a crisp crust. Used on its own, semolina would produce a dense loaf but when combined with wheat flour it gives a light, tender crumb.

YIELD: 1 large round loaf

INGREDIENTS

1 1/4 cups	water
1 tbsp	olive oil
3/4 tsp	salt
1 tsp	sugar
2 cups	white flour*
1 cup	fine semolina flour
1 1/2 tsp	bread-machine or instant yeast

*In Canada use all-purpose or bread flour; in the United States use bread flour.

1. Add all ingredients to machine according to manufacturer's directions. Select dough cycle. When complete remove dough to lightly floured surface; cover and let rest 5 to 10 minutes.

2. Shape into 7-inch round ball and place on lightly greased or parchment-lined baking sheet coated with semolina. Flatten slightly, dust with semolina, cover and let rise in a warm place about 45 to 60 minutes or until doubled in size.

3. Bake at 400°F for 30 to 35 minutes or until crust is golden brown and bottom sounds hollow when tapped (or an instant-read thermometer inserted in center reads 200°F).

ham, onion and walnut kugelhopf

This is a savory version of a buttery sweet raisin and walnut bread that is popular in the Alsace region of France and Germany. These loaves were traditionally baked in round earthenware molds. Today they are often baked in glass or metal molds or tube pans. Enjoy this savory Kugelhopf with salads, soups, or wine and cheese.

YIELD: about 10 servings

INGREDIENTS

3/4 cup	water
1/2 cup	margarine or butter
1 tsp	salt
1 tbsp	sugar
1	large egg
3 cups	white flour*
3 tbsp	instant skim-milk powder
1 tsp	each dried thyme and rubbed sage leaves
1 tbsp	dried onion flakes
1 1/4 tsp	bread-machine or instant yeast
1/2 cup	diced cooked ham
2/3 cup	chopped California walnuts
8–12	California walnut halves

*In Canada use all-purpose or bread flour; in the United States use bread flour.

1. Add all ingredients except ham and walnuts to machine according to manufacturer's directions. Select dough cycle. Add ham and chopped walnuts at ingredient signal (or about 20 to 30 minutes into cycle). When cycle is complete remove dough to lightly floured surface; cover and let rest 10 minutes.

2. Shape dough into circle and make a hole in the middle. Generously butter a 9-inch bundt or tube pan and place walnut halves in indentations in pan. Transfer the ring of dough to the pan, cover and let rise 45 to 60 minutes or until doubled in bulk.

3. Bake at 375°F for 40 to 45 minutes or until golden brown (or an instant-read thermometer inserted in center reads 200°F). Let rest on rack 10 minutes, then unmold and brush with melted butter. Serve at room temperature.

pane alle oliva

Italian bakers make this popular olive bread in many different shapes. This version creates an attractive olive swirl when baked in the oven. However, you can also make a wonderful loaf (that was a favorite with all tasters) by adding the herbs and olives to the dough, shaping it as a baguette and baking it in the oven. Serve this loaf with Italian meals or with tomato or Niçoise salads. If you are pressed for time, make the Quick 'n' Easy version in the bread machine. It makes a great tuna or chicken sandwich.

TIPS
Kalamata and Niçoise olives cured in brine have the best flavor, but pitted canned olives are more convenient. One 14-oz can, drained, yields 1 1/2 cups chopped olives.
For variety, mix green and black olives.

LARGE	INGREDIENTS	EXTRA LARGE
1 1/4 cups	water	1 1/2 cups
1/4 cup	olive oil	6 tbsp
3/4 tsp	salt	1 tsp
3 tbsp	instant skim-milk powder	1/4 cup
1 tsp	sugar	2 tsp
3 cups	white flour*	4 cups
1 1/4 tsp	bread-machine or instant yeast	1 1/2 tsp
1 tsp	each dried oregano and rosemary	1 1/4 tsp
1 1/4 cup	chopped black olives (see Tips)	1 1/2 cups

*In Canada use all-purpose or bread flour; in the United States use bread flour.

VARIATIONS
Baguette
Make dough as directed, but add herbs and olives at ingredient signal (or about 20 to 30 minutes into cycle). You can also knead the herbs and olives into the dough by hand after you take it out of the machine. Shape as directed for baguette on page 17.

Quick 'n' Easy Pane Alle Oliva
Increase flour to 3 1/4 cups for large and 4 1/3 cups for extra large. Decrease olives to 1 cup for large and 1 1/4 cups for extra large. Add all ingredients to machine according to manufacturer's directions. Select basic white bread or French cycle.

1. Select loaf size. Add all ingredients except oregano, rosemary and olives to machine according to manufacturer's directions. Select dough cycle. When cycle is complete, remove dough, cover and let rest 5 to 10 minutes.
2. For a large loaf press or roll dough into 9- x 12-inch rectangle on lightly floured surface; for an extra large loaf divide into 2 pieces and roll into 8- x 10-inch rectangles. Combine herbs and olives and spread over dough leaving a 1-inch border. Roll up tightly from the long side jelly-roll style and pinch edges and ends to seal. Place on lightly greased or parchment-lined baking sheet, tucking ends under, and sift additional corn meal or flour on top. Cover and let rise in a warm place about 45 minutes until almost doubled in size.
3. Using scissors make 7 or 8 deep cuts, about an inch apart down the center of dough exposing some of filling.
4. Bake at 400°F for 30 to 35 minutes or until crust is browned and loaf sounds hollow when tapped (or an instant-read thermometer inserted in center reads 200°F).

european pumpernickel bread

Pumpernickel is a member of the rye family of breads and is related to the German black breads. Traditional pumpernickel has a slightly sweet flavor and is studded with caraway seeds but I found a Russian version made with coarsely ground pepper that pepper lovers favored. It is delicious with cream cheese and it makes a great Rueben sandwich.

LARGE	INGREDIENTS	EXTRA LARGE
1/2 cup	water	1 cup
3/4 cup	low-fat yogurt	3/4 cup
2 tbsp	vegetable oil, margarine or butter	3 tbsp
3/4 tsp	salt	1 tsp
2 tbsp	molasses	3 tbsp
1 3/4 cups	white flour*	2 1/3 cups
1 1/4 cups	rye flour	1 3/4 cups
1/2 cup	natural bakers bran	3/4 cup
1 tsp	instant coffee powder	2 tsp
1 1/2 tbsp	cocoa powder	2 tbsp
1 1/2 tbsp	caraway seeds (optional)	2 tbsp
1 1/4 tsp	bread-machine or instant yeast	1 1/2 tsp

*In Canada use all-purpose or bread flour; in the United States use bread flour.

TIPS

The crust should be crisp and the inside moist. If desired spray loaf with water 2 to 3 times during baking. Commercial ovens have jets of steam to create a crisp crust but this method helps for home baking.

French bakers put dough in bannetons — linen-lined baskets of various shapes — for the final rising before turning the loaves out onto baking sheets. These baskets are expensive to buy but you can achieve a similar result by lining a round 6- to 7-inch wicker basket with a well-floured tea towel; you can even use a well-floured wicker basket or colander without a towel. This technique will create interesting markings on the loaf like those you see in bakeries. Rise your dough in a basket, then carefully turn it out onto a greased or parchment-lined baking sheet, flour side up. Proceed as directed and bake.

VARIATIONS
Russian Rye Bread
Substitute 1/2 to 3/4 tsp coarsely ground pepper for the caraway seeds.

1. Select loaf size. Add ingredients to machine according to manufacturer's directions. Select dough cycle. When cycle is complete, remove dough to lightly floured surface; cover and allow to rest 5 to 10 minutes.
2. Shape dough into round ball and place on lightly greased or parchment-lined baking sheet. Flatten slightly to form a 6- to 7-inch circle. Cover and let rise in a warm place for about 1 hour or until doubled in bulk.

3. Dust generously with white flour. If desired, cut 3 parallel slashes about 1/4 inch deep across the top of loaf; then cut three more slashes in the opposite direction for a criss-cross effect.
4. Place a shallow pan of boiling water on bottom shelf of 400°F oven. Bake for 30 to 35 minutes or until crust is crisp and loaf sounds hollow when tapped (or when an instant-read thermometer inserted in center reads 200°F).

hazelnut and poppy-seed coffee cake

TIPS

If possible, grind poppy seeds in a coffee or spice grinder, a food processor or a blender; if not, you can leave them whole.

If a tube pan is not available, bake in lightly greased 9- x 5-inch loaf pan.

To remove skins from hazelnuts, heat in 350°F oven for 10 minutes or until skins begin to come off. Place in a tea towel a few at a time and rub to remove skins.

VARIATION
Chocolate Streusel Loaf
Substitute orange rind for the lemon rind in dough and omit the poppy seed filling. Roll dough as directed into rectangle. Spread with 2 tbsp softened butter or margarine. Combine 1/2 cup sugar, 2 tbsp cocoa powder and 1/2 cup chopped nuts, and sprinkle over dough. Shape, let rise and bake as directed.

This variation of a traditional Polish poppy-seed bread has hazelnuts in the filling. Hazelnuts (or filberts, as they are often called) are small, sweet and rich. The brown skin can be removed if desired, but it is not necessary. The optional frosting makes this loaf into an attractive centerpiece. Although not traditional, the chocolate variation is popular.

YIELD: 1 large coffee cake (about 12 servings)

	DOUGH
1/2 cup	water
1 cup	low-fat sour cream
2	eggs
2 tbsp	margarine or butter
1/4 cup	sugar
4 cups	white flour*
2 tsp	grated lemon rind
1 1/2 tsp	bread-machine yeast
	FILLING
1/2 cup	poppy seeds, ground (see Tips)
1 cup	finely chopped hazelnuts
1 tbsp	all-purpose flour
1/2 cup	milk
1/3 cup	honey
2 tsp	lemon juice
1 tsp	grated lemon rind
	GLAZE
	1 egg beaten with 1 tbsp water
	FROSTING (optional)
1 cup	confectioners' sugar
1 tbsp	milk, orange juice or lemon juice

*In Canada use all-purpose or bread flour; in the United States use bread flour.

1. Add all dough ingredients to machine according to manufacturer's directions. Select dough cycle.

2. Meanwhile make filling: in small saucepan combine poppy seeds, nuts and flour; stir in milk, honey, lemon juice and rind. Bring to boil, simmer 5 minutes; cool.

3. When cycle is complete, remove dough to lightly floured surface; cover and let rest 5 to 10 minutes.

4. Roll out dough into 20- x 10-inch rectangle. Spread filling over dough and press it in lightly. Tightly roll up along the long side and pinch to seal edges. Place log seam-side down on counter and with sharp knife cut in half lengthwise. Keeping cut side up twist the two halves together. Place cut side up in lightly greased tube pan, overlapping ends and pinching to seal. Cover and let rise in a warm place until almost doubled in bulk, about 45 to 55 minutes.

5. Brush dough areas with glaze. Bake at 350°F for 35 to 45 minutes or until an instant-read thermometer inserted in center reads 200°F; cover with foil during last few minutes if necessary to prevent over-browning. Let stand 5 to 10 minutes before removing from pan. Cool on rack.

6. If frosting is desired, combine confectioners' sugar and milk or juice, mix until smooth and drizzle over loaf.

scandinavian coffee cake

TIP

It takes 8 cardamom pods to yield 1/2 tsp ground cardamom — this is the reason it is so expensive. Use this coffee cake as a centerpiece at a coffee party or brunch.

VARIATION
Holiday Christmas Wreath
Omit cardamom. For filling, substitute candied mixed peel and candied red and green cherries for the apricots and prunes, omit cloves and nutmeg, and increase cinnamon to 2 tsp. Shape, let rise and bake as directed. Omit confectioners' sugar and drizzle with frosting made by mixing 1 cup confectioners' sugar with 1 tbsp milk or lemon juice and 1/4 tsp grated lemon rind. Decorate with candied red and green cherry halves.

Prunes (which are dried plums) have always been popular in Northern Europe since they can be stored easily. They are now regaining popularity elsewhere because they contain antioxidants. This attractive coffee cake is shaped like a Swedish tea ring that my mother made when I was growing up. Cardamom, a member of the ginger family, has a pungent aroma and a spicy sweet flavor. Make the wreath variation for the Christmas season.

	DOUGH
3/4 cup	water
1/4 cup	margarine or butter
1	large egg
3/4 tsp	salt
1/3 cup	sugar
1/2 tsp	cardamom
3 cups	white flour*
1 1/4 tsp	bread-machine or instant yeast
	FILLING
1 1/2 tbsp	butter or margarine, softened
1/2 cup	brown sugar, packed
1 1/2 tsp	cinnamon
1/4 tsp	each cloves and nutmeg
3/4 cup	each finely diced apricots and prunes
1/4 cup	finely chopped almonds
	GLAZE
	1 egg yolk beaten with 1 tbsp milk
	TOPPING
	confectioners' sugar

*In Canada use all-purpose or bread flour; in the United States use bread flour.

1. Add all dough ingredients to machine according to manufacturer's directions. Select dough cycle. When cycle is complete, remove dough to lightly floured surface; cover and let rest 5 to 10 minutes.

2. Pat or roll dough into 18- x 9-inch rectangle and spread with softened butter. In small bowl mix together brown sugar, cloves, nutmeg, apricots, prunes and almonds, and sprinkle evenly over dough. Roll up dough from long side jelly-roll style and pinch edges together to seal.

3. With seam side down, shape into a circle on a large lightly greased or parchment-lined baking sheet or pizza pan; overlap ends and pinch to seal. With sharp knife or scissors cut 2/3 of way into ring at 1-inch intervals. Turn each section on its side, cut side up. Cover and let rise in a warm place for 45 to 60 minutes or until doubled in bulk.

4. Brush dough with glaze. Bake at 375°F for 25 to 30 minutes or until golden brown (or an instant-read thermometer inserted in center reads 200°F). Cool on rack. Sift confectioners' sugar on top just before serving.

mardis gras coffee cake

This cake makes a wonderful centerpiece to share with family and friends at Easter as well as during Mardis Gras festivities.

YIELD: 1 large coffee cake, about 12 servings

DOUGH

1 1/4 cups	milk
1/2 cup	margarine or butter
4	egg yolks
1 tsp	salt
1/4 cup	sugar
4 cups	white flour*
1 tsp	each ground nutmeg and grated lemon rind
1 1/2 tsp	bread-machine or instant yeast

FILLING

1 pkg (8 oz/250g)	cream cheese, softened
1/2 cup	confectioners' sugar
1/2 tsp	vanilla
3/4 cup	coarsely chopped pecans

FROSTING

2 cups	confectioners' sugar
3 tbsp	milk, orange or lemon juice
	purple, yellow and green coarse sugar or sprinkles

*In Canada use all-purpose or bread flour; in the United States use bread flour.

TIPS

To help hold the ring shape, grease the outside of an empty coffee can, place in middle of baking sheet and shape the dough around it. Remove can immediately after baking.

King's cake is a traditional crown-shaped coffee cake that is shared by family, friends and revelers in New Orleans at Mardi Gras festivities. According to tradition, a tiny baby doll is hidden inside the bread after baking. Whoever finds it is crowned king or queen and hosts the next party.

The Mardis Gras colors are gold for power, green for faith and purple for justice.

1. Add all dough ingredients to machine according to manufacturer's directions. Select dough cycle. When cycle is complete, remove dough to lightly floured surface; cover and let rest 5 to 10 minutes.
2. Roll dough into 30- x 5-inch rectangle. Beat cream cheese, confectioners' sugar and vanilla together until smooth. Spread lengthwise down the center of rectangle and sprinkle pecans on top. Fold both sides of dough over filling and overlapping; pinch to seal edges. Form dough into a circle on lightly greased or parchment-lined 12-inch pizza pan or baking sheet, overlapping and pinching the ends to seal. Cover and let rise about 45 minutes or until doubled in size.
3. Slash the dough about every 2 inches, going deep enough to expose the filling. Bake in 375°F oven for 30 minutes or until golden brown (or an instant-read thermometer inserted in center reads 200°F). Cool on rack.
4. For frosting, mix confectioners' sugar and milk or juice together until smooth and spread over crown. Decorate with colored sugar sprinkles in wide strips of alternating colors.

bumbleberry coffee cake

Bumbleberry, one of my favorite flavors, isn't a berry — it's a combination that includes some or all of blackberries, strawberries, cranberries, blueberries and cherries.

YIELD: 1 coffee cake or 12 slices

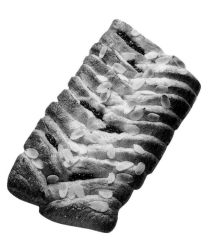

DOUGH	
3/4 cup	milk
1	large egg
1/2 cup	margarine or butter
3/4 tsp	salt
3 tbsp	sugar
3 cups	white flour*
1/2 tsp	ground cinnamon
1 1/4 tsp	bread-machine or instant yeast
FILLING	
1 1/2 cups	raspberries, fresh or frozen
1/4 cup	water
1/4 cup	sugar
4 tsp	cornstarch
1/3 cup	each dried cranberries, dried blueberries and dried cherries

*In Canada use all-purpose or bread flour; in the United States use bread flour.

TIPS

Berries are high in fiber and vitamin C.

If one dried fruit is not available, double one of the others, or add apple, rhubarb or plums.

If a flat baking sheet without sides is not available, then roll and shape the loaf on parchment paper on the counter and carefully transfer it to the baking sheet.

Wrap any leftovers securely; freeze.

1. Add all dough ingredients to machine according to manufacturer's directions. Select dough cycle.
2. Meanwhile combine raspberries and water in small saucepan and bring to boil. Mix sugar and cornstarch together and stir into raspberries; bring to boil for 1 minute to thicken, stirring constantly. Remove from heat, stir in dried fruits, then cover and set aside to cool.
3. When cycle is complete, remove dough to lightly floured surface; cover and let rest 5 to 10 minutes.

4. Roll out dough on lightly greased flat baking sheet into a 13- x 10-inch rectangle and spread the filling down the center of dough in a 3-inch-wide strip. Using scissors, make horizontal cuts in the dough on either side of the filling (from the outside edge to the edge of the filling), about 1 inch apart. Starting at one end, fold the first strip on the right side diagonally over the filling, then fold over the first strip on the left side so that it overlaps the first. Continue with the remaining strips

of dough. Cover and let rise in a warm place for 35 to 40 minutes or until doubled in bulk.
5. Bake at 375°F for 20 to 25 minutes or until golden brown or an instant-read thermometer reads 200°F. Cover with foil during last 5 to 10 minutes if necessary to prevent over-browning. Brush warm bread with milk and sprinkle with sugar.

greek easter ring

TIP

With slight variations you can make other traditional Easter favorites (such as Hot Cross Buns). See variations on page 141.

My husband and I enjoyed this traditional bread on a visit to the Greek islands a few years ago at Easter. It was served with their wonderful yogurt and honey.

YIELD: 1 coffee cake (about 12 servings)

	DOUGH
1 cup	water
3 tbsp	margarine or butter
2	eggs
1 tsp	salt
1/4 cup	sugar
4 cups	white flour*
1/4 cup	instant skim-milk powder
2 tsp	grated lemon rind
1 1/2 tsp	anise seeds
1 1/2 tsp	bread-machine or instant yeast
	GLAZE
	1 egg beaten with 1 tbsp water
	TOPPING
	sesame seeds

*In Canada use all-purpose or bread flour; in the United States use bread flour.

1. Add all dough ingredients to machine according to manufacturer's directions. Select dough cycle. When cycle is complete, remove dough to lightly floured surface; cover and let rest 5 to 10 minutes.
2. Cut dough in half and roll each piece into a 32-inch rope. Twist the 2 ropes together and form into a circle on a lightly greased or parchment-lined baking sheet. Join and overlap the ends and pinch them together to seal. Cover and allow to rise in a warm place until almost doubled in bulk, about 35 to 40 minutes.
3. Brush with glaze and sprinkle with sesame seeds. Bake at 375°F for 30 to 35 minutes. Cool on rack.

more easter breads

Many countries and cultures have special breads or buns for this Christian holiday, and most of them use eggs — the symbol of rebirth. The variations here are based on the dough for Greek Easter Ring. Easter symbols include the ring or circle shape, representing the unity of families, and the cross. Enjoy these flavorful coffee cakes for breakfast, brunch or with tea.

Russian Easter Ring
Substitute 1 tbsp brandy for lemon rind and anise seed. At ingredient signal (or about 20 to 30 minutes into cycle) add 1/4 cup chopped toasted almonds, 1/4 cup golden raisins and 1/2 cup candied pineapple. Shape and let rise. Glaze, sprinkle with sesame seeds or sliced almonds if desired and bake as directed.

Italian Easter Ring
Increase lemon rind to 3 tbsp. Omit anise seeds, glaze and topping. Shape and let rise as directed. Meanwhile prepare topping by mixing 1/4 tsp cinnamon, 3 tbsp sugar, 3/4 cup chopped toasted almonds or pine nuts and 1 egg yolk. Spread topping on ring just before baking and bake as directed.

Hot Cross Buns
Yield: *16 buns*
Add 2 tsp grated orange rind, 1/2 tsp ground cloves and 1/4 tsp ground ginger with the flour. Substitute 1 tsp ground cinnamon for the anise seeds. At ingredient signal add 1/3 cup each of golden raisins and currants.

Divide dough into 16 pieces, shape each into a smooth ball and place 2 inches apart on lightly greased or parchment-lined baking sheets. Cover and allow to rise in a warm place until almost doubled, about 40 minutes. Brush with glaze but omit sesame seeds.

If desired make a thick batter to pipe crosses on buns with pastry bag. For batter, mix 3/4 cup all-purpose flour and 1/2 tsp baking powder with 8 to 9 tbsp milk (or enough to form a thick batter). Bake at 375°F for 12 to 15 minutes. Cool on rack. If crosses were not piped on before baking, mix 1 cup confectioners' sugar with 1 tbsp milk or lemon juice and spoon or pipe onto buns in the form of a cross.

christstollen

The fruit and nuts in this rich German Christmas bread help keep it moist and fresh longer than other breads. According to one tradition, the folded shape represents the blanket laid over the baby Jesus, and the confectioners' sugar on top represents snow. If time is at a premium make the quick variation.
YIELD: 1 large coffee cake (about 10 servings)

1. Add all dough ingredients except raisins, peel, cherries and walnuts to machine according to manufacturer's directions. Select dough cycle. Add fruits and nuts at ingredient signal (or about 20 to 30 minutes into cycle). When cycle is complete, remove dough to lightly floured surface; cover and let rest 5 to 10 minutes.
2. Roll into 13- x 10-inch oval and fold over lengthwise, not quite in half, leaving 1 inch of bottom layer extending beyond the top. Press lightly to seal and place on lightly greased or parchment-lined baking sheet. Cover and let rise in warm place about 40 to 45 minutes.
3. Brush with glaze. Bake in 350°F oven for 45 to 50 minutes or until browned (or an instant-read thermometer inserted in the center reads 200°F). Sift confectioners' sugar generously on top.

	DOUGH
1 cup	water
1/4 cup	margarine or butter
1	egg
2 tbsp	brandy or rum*
3/4 tsp	salt
1	orange, grated rind only
1/4 cup	brown or white sugar
3 tbsp	instant skim-milk powder
2 cups	white flour**
1 1/3 cups	whole-wheat flour
1 1/4 tsp	bread-machine or instant yeast
1/2 cup	golden raisins
1/2 cup	chopped candied orange and lemon peel
1/3 cup	whole candied green and red cherries
1/2 cup	toasted California walnuts (see tips)
	GLAZE
1 egg white or yolk beaten with 1 tbsp water	
	TOPPING
confectioners' sugar	

*If desired substitute 1 egg yolk or 2 tbsp orange juice plus 1 tsp brandy or rum extract for the brandy or rum. (Save the egg white for glaze.)
**In Canada use all-purpose or bread flour; in the United States use bread flour.

more christmas breads

A number of Christmas breads from around the world use similar doughs but vary in flavor and shape. I have based this collection of breads on the dough recipe for Christstollen. Don't limit these breads to the holidays — they are great for any gathering. You can also wrap them up in cellophane for gifts or make smaller ones to include in a gift basket with special teas or coffees.

VARIATIONS

Dutch Christmas Bread

Substitute white flour for the whole-wheat, orange juice for the brandy, 1/2 cup candied mixed fruits for the candied peel and currants for the cherries. Add 1/2 tsp each of nutmeg and mace and omit the walnuts.

Prepare dough as directed. Meanwhile in food processor, combine 3/4 cup toasted almonds, 2 tbsp brown sugar, 1 egg white, 1 tbsp butter or margarine and 1/2 tsp almond extract and process until finely chopped for filling. Roll dough into oval shape and spread filling over one half of dough, leaving a 1-inch border. Fold other half of dough over filling and pinch seams firmly to seal. Place on lightly greased or parchment-lined baking sheet; let rise as directed. Brush with glaze and sprinkle with sliced or slivered almonds if desired. Bake as directed and sprinkle with confectioners' sugar if desired.

Portuguese Epiphany Ring

Substitute port for the brandy and pine nuts for walnuts and omit peel and cherries in original recipe. Add grated zest of 1 lemon. Prepare dough as directed. Roll out dough into an 18- x 9-inch rectangle then roll up the long side jelly-roll style and pinch ends to seal. Place on lightly greased or parchment-lined baking sheet and shape into a circle, joining and overlapping the ends. Let rise, brush dough with glaze as directed and decorate with candied cherries or fruit. Bake as directed. Heat 2 tbsp apricot jam and brush on warm loaf.

Swedish Christmas Bread

Substitute 1/2 cup citron peel for the cherries and nuts in original recipe. Omit brandy and add 1 tsp cardamom. Prepare dough as directed. Shape dough into smooth ball by drawing dough down and under and pinching it together underneath. Place smooth side up on lightly greased or parchment-lined baking sheet and pat with palm of hand, smoothing out and pressing down slightly. Let rise, brush dough with glaze and bake as directed. Cool on rack. Place paper snowflake design or doily on top of loaf, sift confectioners' sugar on top, then remove paper.

Czech Christmas Braid

Substitute 1/4 cup each of candied fruit peel and slivered almonds for the peel, cherries and nuts in the original recipe. Omit brandy and add 1/4 tsp each of ginger and mace or nutmeg.

Prepare dough as directed. Roll dough into 9-inch log. Divide and braid as directed for double or single braided Challah (page 125). Let rise, brush with glaze as directed, decorate with slivered or sliced almonds and bake. Cool on rack and sprinkle generously with confectioners' sugar.

Quick 'n' Easy Christmas Loaf

Omit brandy or juice and substitute 1/3 cup each of currants, whole candied cherries and mixed peel for the raisins, peel, cherries and nuts in original recipe. Select sweet or basic white cycle.

chapter eight

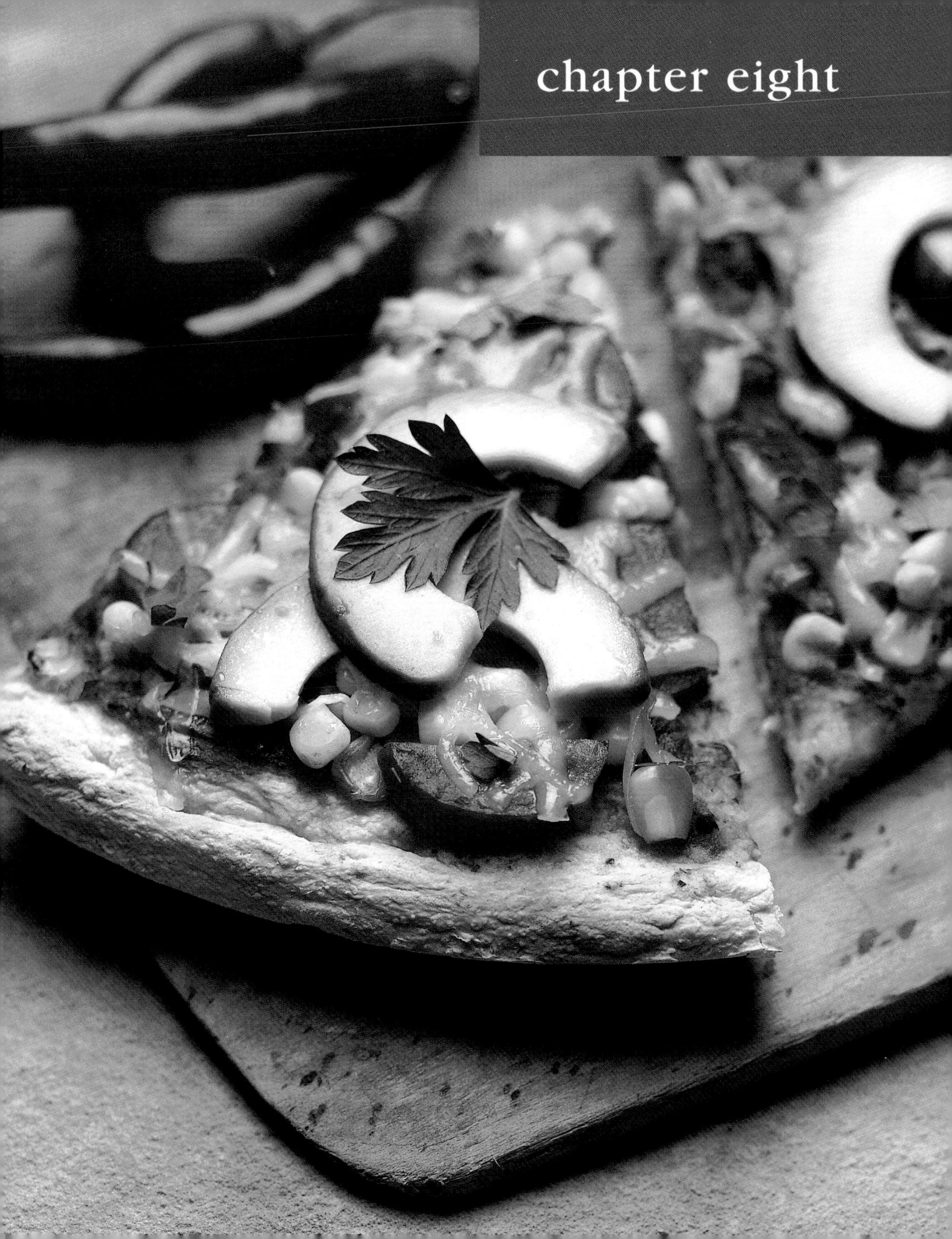

more hints for successful baking

about ingredients

techniques and tips

answers to frequently asked questions

This chapter provides additional information about ingredients and tips on storing breads. For new bakers, I have included dough-handling techniques for the recipes in chapters 5, 6 and 7. Finally, there are answers to a number of frequently asked questions that I have received from consumers, and a guide for easily adapting your favorite recipes to the bread machine.

about ingredients

FLOUR

Wheat flour is the main ingredient used in bread, and North America produces some of the finest wheat in the world. Since brands and types of flour differ from region to region, it is worth the time to experiment with several kinds. Be sure to keep notes as to your preferences. One important note of caution: do not use self-rising flour or cake flour for bread-machine recipes.

Canadian all-purpose white flour is a mixture of hard wheat and soft wheat. The high percentage of hard wheat gives this all-purpose flour a high gluten or protein content, making it ideal for bread baking. American all-purpose flour has less gluten; use bread flour instead.

White flours can lose moisture and gluten content during long or improper storage even if the bag is not open. Store white flour in airtight containers at room temperature and use it up within 8 to 12 months. To extend the shelf life up to two years, freeze it in airtight plastic containers.

Whole-wheat flour is more nutritious than white flour because it contains the entire wheat grain, including the wheat germ and the bran. Since wheat germ is prone to spoilage, whole-wheat flour should be used within 3 to 6 months if it is stored at room temperature. It can be frozen in airtight plastic containers for up to a year. Whole-wheat flour adds fiber to bread and gives it a nutty taste. A whole-wheat loaf is usually heavier and denser and the dough also takes longer to rise.

Canadian specialty bread-flour blends are readily available in Canada and will give a larger volume and lighter texture than Canadian all-purpose or whole-wheat flour. You should experiment with these blends. Some people find that a bread made with white bread-flour blends and bread-machine yeast is a little too light, but a whole-wheat or rye bread-flour blend can produce a light-textured yet somewhat substantial loaf.

Other flours and grains — such as rolled oats, cornmeal, bran, cracked wheat, rye, barley and spelt — provide flavor and texture but they should be added in smaller proportions since they are low in gluten. You can also use gluten flour to add structure if needed. Specialty milled flours may also be available at a mill in your area. Freshly milled flours may give a sweeter taste, but because they are often coarser than commercial flours the gluten may not develop as well, resulting in heavier, lower-volume breads.

My preference and recommendation for the recipes in this book in Canada is to start out with all-purpose flour and bread-machine yeast. Then you can experiment with specialty bread flours using either bread-machine or instant yeast and decide which textures you like and which volumes best suit your machine.

In the United States you should use bread flour, which has a higher gluten or protein content, rather than American all-purpose flour. Since American bread flours do not have the same amount of gluten as Canadian flours the recipe quantities may require some adjustments. Each type of flour performs and reacts differently in combination with other ingredients, so there is no general rule. However, the higher-gluten Canadian flours absorb more water, so I recommend reducing the water in the recipe and adding the remaining amount gradually if needed. If you forget to cut back on the water you can add flour, a tablespoon at a time, as needed. Be sure to make notes on the recipe about your adjustments.

You can also give more strength and structure to American flours by adding gluten.

GLUTEN

The gluten in flour develops elasticity when combined with liquids. This elasticity allows the dough to stretch and trap air bubbles given off by yeast. Gluten can be added to flours that are low in gluten to increase the strength and structure of the dough. Commercial gluten is available in two forms: vital gluten, which is pure gluten, and gluten flour, which is a mixture of gluten and flour. For American flours (which have a lower gluten content than Canadian flours) you should add about 1 tsp vital gluten per cup of whole-wheat flour. If you are using gluten flour, you will obviously have to add a little more, but since the gluten content of commercial gluten flours is variable, it may take some experimentation to achieve the desired results.

YEAST

Yeast is a living organism that, when moistened by a liquid, fed with sugar and warmed carefully, will produce the carbon dioxide that makes dough rise. Bread-machine yeast also contains ascorbic acid to improve the performance of the yeast. Fast-acting yeasts (such as instant, rapid-rise or quick-rise) that are formulated to blend with dry ingredients can also be used in bread-machine recipes. I recommend buying yeast in a jar or can because it is easy to measure out what you need and reseal the container. A few recipes use the same amount of yeast for both the large and the extra-large loaves. It is best to start with the amount recommended in the recipe and adjust it later if needed for your machine or the flours you are using.

For best results use fresh, dry yeast. Check the freshness date on container before purchasing. Yeast can be stored for up to four months in the refrigerator; keep it at the back so it will not be affected by drafts or fluctuating temperatures near the door.

LIQUIDS

In a yeast dough, liquids bind the ingredients together, allow the gluten to develop structure and elasticity and sometimes add flavor. Make sure the liquid is at the temperature recommended in the manufacturer's manual — usually tepid or room temperature except for super-rapid or express cycles. Different liquids give different crusts. Water gives a crisper crust. If the water in your area is very hard add 1 tsp lemon juice or vinegar to make a more acidic environment for the yeast.

Milk gives a softer crust and texture. I recommend using dry milk powder for two reasons: it avoids the bother of heating liquid milk, and it provides another medium for the yeast to feed on. Powdered milk also allows you to use milk recipes on the delay-start cycle without fear of spoilage (as long as no other perishable ingredients are used). If you substitute fresh milk for dry milk powder and water, warm the milk for a few seconds in the microwave.

Buttermilk gives a tangy flavor and a tender crumb. The recipes in this book use buttermilk powder, but if you have fresh buttermilk on hand, you can substitute it for powder and water; warm it for a few seconds in the microwave. If you have fresh buttermilk left over, freeze it in small quantities; thaw and shake before using. If you don't have fresh or powdered buttermilk you can create a substitute: mix 1 tbsp lemon juice or vinegar and 1 cup milk and allow to stand 5 minutes.

Fruit or vegetable juices can replace water and add wonderful flavors. It is also important to remember that fresh fruits and vegetables will add moisture so liquids need to be reduced. As a general rule, cut back liquid by 1/2 cup for every cup of fruit or vegetable.

Beer can also replace water, especially in whole-wheat and rye breads. Dark beers give the most flavor. Unless the beer is already flat, pour it into a measuring cup and allow it to sit at room temperature for a while.

FATS

Fats add flavor and moisten the gluten. They also slow down moisture loss in bread; breads that do not contain fat will go stale quickly. Butter, margarine, shortening and oil can all be successfully interchanged in these recipes. Butter or olive oil may be chosen for their special flavors while specific types of soft margarine or oil may be preferred for particular diets. I like oil or soft margarine for ease of measuring. Calorie-reduced margarine or butter can be used, but since they have added water you may need to cut back on liquids. For special diets you can experiment by reducing the fat and increasing the liquid or by replacing some of the fat with fruit purées such as applesauce and reducing the liquid.

SWEETENERS

Sweeteners feed the yeast. They also add flavor, give the crust a golden color and help prevent the bread from drying out. The recipes in this book have been developed using granulated white sugar unless otherwise indicated. White and brown sugar are interchangeable but they differ in color and flavor. Low-calorie sweeteners can also be substituted; experiment with varying amounts until you find the desired degree of sweetness. Powdered confectioners' sugar should not to be used as a sweetener in bread because it contains cornstarch; however it can be used in frosting recipes.

If you substitute a "wet" sweetener (such as molasses or honey) for sugar you will likely need to reduce the liquids by the same quantity. Dark honey and molasses give the most distinctive flavor. If honey has crystallized in the bottom of a jar, place the jar in a pan of hot water or microwave it for a few seconds. Keep honey or molasses in plastic squeeze bottles for easier measuring.

EGGS

Eggs add richness, color and volume to bread. All the recipes in this book were tested with large eggs. Eggs have an effect on the texture and volume of bread. You can substitute 1/4 cup water for 1 egg, but the bread will have a heavier texture and lower volume. In the reverse situation, to lighten a heavy bread, substitute an egg for 1/4 cup water. To lower fat and cholesterol, you can substitute 2 egg whites or 1/4 cup egg substitute for 1 egg. The downside of using eggs is that sometimes breads containing eggs dry out faster. Also, you can't make them on the delay-start cycle.

SALT

Salt strengthens the gluten structure, prevents the yeast from over-rising and brings out the flavor of other ingredients. I have used low quantities of salt in most of the recipes in this book and have added a salt-free bread for special diets. You can use a salt substitute as long as it contains enough sodium to have an effect on the yeast. It is important to keep the salt away from the yeast when adding the ingredients, especially on the delay cycle. For this reason salt is placed near the top with the liquids in the ingredient lists.

DRIED FRUITS, NUTS AND SEEDS

Dried fruits and nuts provide flavor and texture. Usually it is best to add them at the ingredient signal or raisin/nut beep during the kneading so they won't be completely pulverized or puréed. If your machine does not have an ingredient signal or raisin/nut beep, check the instruction manual, calculate the starting time of the second kneading and set a timer. In most machines this point is 20 to 30 minutes into the cycle. If you will be away from the machine during the kneading process, you will have to add all the ingredients at the beginning. If this is the case, freeze the dried fruit and use larger pieces of nuts (so they won't break down as quickly). You can freeze dried fruit in a single layer on a baking sheet, then seal it in airtight plastic bags.

If you find that raisins or dates clump together at the bottom of the bread pan, try air-drying them overnight on a counter so they are not as moist or sticky. Chopped dates that are coated in dextrose are also available and are very convenient. Although they are a little sweeter, I find they stay better distributed in the dough. If you substitute dried fruit for fresh (for example in Blueberry Swirl Sourcream Bread, page 64), you will need to increase the liquids. Nuts or dried fruits can often be omitted unless they provide a key flavor or they represent an important element of a traditional recipe (for example, in recipes for breads served for special occasions or on religious holidays).

Because nuts and seeds contain natural oils that can turn rancid, they should not be stored at room temperature for an extended period of time; store them in the refrigerator or freezer. To intensify the nut flavors you can toast nuts in a 350°F oven for 8 to 10 minutes. Alternatively, toast them in a non-stick skillet over medium heat until golden brown, shaking or stirring often. But beware — nuts can burn easily if left unattended!

HERBS AND DRIED VEGETABLES

These seasonings add a multitude of flavor. I recommend dried herbs since fresh herbs add moisture. However, if you use fresh herbs, triple the amount and adjust the consistency of the dough if necessary. I also recommend using dried onion both for convenience and to avoid extra moisture, but you can substitute 1/4 cup diced fresh onion for 1 tbsp dried onion and reduce the liquid by 1 to 2 tbsp.

techniques and tips

HANDLING DOUGH

The recipes in chapters 5, 6 and 7 are for doughs that are made in the bread machine and shaped by hand and baked in the oven.

After making the dough in the bread machine, remove it with floured hands to a surface sprinkled with 1 to 2 tbsp flour. Shape the dough into a smooth ball by pulling it down the sides and underneath, cover it with a clean tea towel, plastic wrap or lightly greased wax paper and leave it to rest and relax.

Some doughs will be stickier than others. If the dough is too sticky to handle or shape, knead in a little more flour.

Kneading is quite simple. Fold the dough in half toward you, then push it away with the heel of your hand. Give it a quarter turn and repeat 2 or 3 times. Many people who have made bread by hand still like to have the feeling of kneading the dough — it's great therapy after a stressful day!

Once any extra flour is added and the dough has been left to rest for a few minutes, it's ready to be shaped as directed in recipes.

If something comes up and you can't shape the dough when it's ready, just punch it down in the bread pan, close the lid and let it rise another hour. Dough is very

forgiving and the extra rise will just improve the texture. You can also slow down a rising dough in the refrigerator (see below).

REFRIGERATING DOUGH

If you don't have time to shape the dough when the bread machine cycle is finished, you can store it sealed in airtight bags in the refrigerator for 1 to 2 days to slow down the rising. About 1 to 1 1/2 hours before you are ready to use the dough, punch it down and bring it to room temperature. Then you can shape it, let it rise and bake it according to the recipe. You can also shape the dough into loaves or rolls before refrigerating and cover with plastic wrap. Bring the loaves to room temperature, then let them rise and bake according to directions. With this method, you can prepare dough in the morning for fresh rolls at dinner or refrigerate loaves overnight to bake in the morning

for breakfast. It is also handy if when you want to make a loaf with two flavors or braid two or three different types of dough together (for example, Classic White and Tomato-pepper, or Challah and Black Forest) to shape and bake as directed for Challah Bread (page 125).

FREEZING DOUGH

If you don't have time to shape and bake your dough within two days you can feeze it, sealed in airtight bags, for up to 3 months. Remove frozen dough from freezer the night before you need it, and thaw it in the refrigerator or at room temperature for 2 to 6 hours (depending on size). When the dough is thawed, shape it and let it rise (rising may take longer if the dough is cold). This method is handy for unused pizza dough or for an occasion when you want to make a variety of different kinds of dough but bake them all at the same time.

RISING DOUGH

Once the dough has been shaped, it should be covered again with wax paper or a clean tea towel and left to rise. Doughs should not expand more than double their size in this last rise or the gluten structure will give way and the loaves will collapse. Rising dough needs a warm (75°F to 80°F) draft-free place.

I suggest the following areas:

1. on top of refrigerator;
2. in a sunny window;
3. on top of pan of hot tap water;
4. on top of a heating pad turned to the lowest temperature setting;
5. in a warm oven (turn oven on to 200°F for 1 minute and then turn off).

FINISHING DOUGH

Melted butter, margarine or oil brushed on the shaped dough before rising will prevent the dough from drying out and make it brown more quickly.

After the dough has risen, liquids can be brushed on the top before baking to give different finishes. Here are some suggestions:

1. water gives a crisp crust;
2. milk gives a glossy darker finish;
3. whole egg mixed with 1 tbsp water or milk gives a shiny medium brown finish;
4. egg white and 1 tbsp water gives shiny lighter finish;
5. egg yolk and 1 tbsp water or milk gives a shiny darker brown finish.

OVEN BAKING DOUGH

Bread pans should be lightly greased. Rub the pan or brush it lightly with softened margarine, butter, shortening or oil, or spray it with oil or non-stick cooking spray. Baking sheets may also be lined with parchment paper.

Generally it is best to bake bread or rolls one pan at a time, in the middle of oven, but if you are pressed for time you can bake two pans in the upper third and lower third of oven; reverse and rotate the positions of the pans half way through baking time.

To give a crisp crust to certain breads such as French, Ciabatta, Pane alle Oliva or Pane di Semola, place a pan of hot water on the bottom shelf to create steam. Spraying the oven and dough with water will also help to create a crisper crust.

If breads or coffee cakes brown too quickly, cover them with foil during last 10 or 15 minutes; thick, dense items may not be cooked in the middle even though the crust is browned.

Loaves and crusty buns are done when they have a hollow sound if tapped on the bottom or when an instant-read thermometer inserted in the center reads 200°F.

Light, shiny pans give lighter crusts. If dark or glass pans give too dark a crust, then reduce the oven temperature by 25°F. It also helps to line dark pans with parchment paper.

BAKING BREAD-MACHINE RECIPES IN THE OVEN

The recipes in Chapters 1, 2, 3 and 4 can be made as dough and hand shaped. To make a regular large loaf in a loaf pan, roll or press the dough into a rectangle, the short side of which is about the length of the pan. Roll the dough jelly-roll style from the short side into a log. Pinch the edges to seal and place the log seam-side down in a greased 9- x 5-inch pan. For an extra-large batch divide the dough into two pieces, roll each piece into a log and place in two greased 8 1/2- x 4 1/2-inch pans. Let the loaves rise until almost doubled in bulk and bake at 400°F for about 30 minutes. The bread is done when the crust is golden brown or when an instant-read thermometer inserted in the center reads 200°F. To make free-form loaves, shape the dough into rounds or oblongs, place on lightly greased or parchment-lined baking sheets or pizza pans, let rise, and bake.

HANDLING BAKED BREAD

If possible remove breads from baking pans promptly after baking and cool on wire racks to prevent the crusts from going soggy. Some bread machines have a cooling cycle or a keep-warm cycle, but I have found that breads with tender, soft textures (especially those containing fruit or vegetables) may cave in on the sides if they are left in the machine after baking.

If you have trouble removing bread from the bread-machine pan, wait for five minutes and try again; sometimes it will come out more easily. You can also rap the edge of pan on a padded surface or a wooden cutting board. If necessary use a rubber spatula to help loosen the loaf; never use a metal utensil as it will damage the non-stick coating of the pan. Next time, try spraying the paddle and the interior of the bread pan lightly with a non-stick cooking spray. If the paddle sticks in the bread, cut around it with a small knife and pry it loose with a fork, knife, small pliers or tweezers. Don't give away a loaf with the paddle still in it — believe me, we have done it!

For a softer crust, brush warm breads with softened or melted butter or margarine immediately after baking. For a sweeter finish that will also soften the crust, brush on a mixture of equal portions of water and honey, maple syrup or molasses.

Allow bread to cool for at least 15 minutes before slicing. Most loaves will be easier to slice after cooling for an hour but some tender and moist loaves should cool for even longer.

Slicing fresh bread can be difficult so it is important to use a good serrated bread knife or an electric knife. Some bread knives have a wire guide for thickness and look like a fiddle bow — I have one that has an adjustable metal guide. Some people use an electric food slicer for bread. You can also cut bread into various shapes (such as wedges, triangles or narrow strips), break it into chunks or cut it with cookie cutters.

Cutting boards with slats on top are also popular. When you slice the bread, crumbs are caught in the box below. These boards are especially convenient to use at the table.

STORING AND REHEATING BREAD

Homemade breads do not keep as long as commercial store-bought breads because they do not contain preservatives. If possible, store bread at room temperature. Most breads (with the exception of gluten-free varieties) will stale faster in the refrigerator. Breads will usually remain fresh and moist for two or three days; breads containing fruit and fats will stay moist longer, but breads containing eggs tend to dry out sooner. If you know you will not use bread within a day of baking, it may be best to wrap the loaf and freeze it while it is still fresh.

Cool bread completely before wrapping for storage. To keep the crust crispy, leave bread open on the counter or store it in a paper or cotton bag. To soften the crust and keep the bread fresh longer, store it in a plastic bag. To keep bread for an extended time, wrap it airtight in foil, plastic wrap or plastic bags and freeze it for up to 3 months. For freezing I like to cut the loaf in half or slice it and individually wrap the slices. This way I don't have to defrost the whole loaf and I have the opportunity to enjoy a variety of breads throughout the day. Bread can be thawed at room temperature or wrapped in foil and placed in a 275°F oven for 25 to 30 minutes (depending on the size of the loaf).

To re-crisp the crust, place the loaf in a dampened paper bag and heat in moderate oven. To reheat or freshen stale bread, wrap it in foil and heat in a 250°F oven until warm.

answers to frequently asked questions

Why doesn't my loaf turn out the same every time I make it?
If the flour or the yeast is old or has not been stored properly you can get poor results. On hot, humid days the extra humidity in the air might make the dough stickier or cause the bread to overflow the pan. Conversely, if the room is colder than usual, or if the bread machine is sitting in the draft from a ceiling fan or an air conditioner, the cooler temperature will also affect the results. Remember that even if the appearance of your loaf is not perfect, the chances are ten to one that it will taste just fine, and will probably make great toast!

Why aren't all my loaves the same height or as tall as those of my friends?
Big is not always best! Although a tall loaf is impressive, it may not have the texture that everyone wants. The difference in rising times for various cycles for different brands of machines can affect the height. If you use the rapid (2 to 3 hour) cycles your loaves will have slightly less height. In fact the super-rapid cycles now available on some machines give smaller volumes and need specially designed recipes. Some ingredients such as whole grains, low-gluten flours or special grinds of flour can give a lower volume, and different types of flours and yeast can also affect

the height. Incorrect measuring of flour can also affect both the height and the texture. If you end up with a heavy texture, be creative and call it a flatbread! Broil or grill slices to use as a base for spreads or open-face sandwiches.

Why do some extra-large loaves use the same amount of yeast or egg as a large loaf?
In some recipes we found that with certain combinations of ingredients the same quantities of yeast and egg worked equally well for both loaf sizes.

When should I use the whole-wheat cycle?
The longer rising time of the whole-wheat cycle is preferable for 100% whole-wheat or grain breads. If that cycle is not available or you are in a hurry, you can use the basic white cycle but the loaf will have a lower volume. (You might try increasing the yeast slightly.) If half or less than half of the total flour in a recipe is either whole-wheat or a whole-wheat blend, the basic white cycle will be quite satisfactory.

Do all the ingredients have to be at room temperature?
For best results most manufacturers recommend that the ingredients be at room temperature, although some machines have a warming or pre-heating cycle that eliminates

this need. It only takes a few seconds to warm ingredients in the micro-wave. If you are not in a hurry, just load the ingredients into the machine and select the delay-start cycle to begin mixing 30 minutes later. I have successfully made all these recipes in the machines I used for testing without warming ingredients such as eggs, yogurt, sour cream or cottage cheese, so experiment with your machine.

Why did I end up with a "door stop" or a "hockey puck"?
Perhaps you forgot the yeast! Believe me, we have all done it. To avoid this, assemble all ingredients near the pan before starting and put each container aside after you add the ingredient. Checking off ingredients on the recipe as you add them can also be helpful. The wrong quantity of flour or liquids that are too hot can also affect the yeast.

Why did the loaf touch the top of the machine or form a mushroom top?
The quantity of ingredients may have exceeded the recommended volume for your machine, or the flour-and-yeast combination you chose may have given too high a rise. Perhaps you forgot the salt (which controls the yeast), or you added too many sweet ingredients (older dried fruit has more sugar) to an already sweet dough. Next time, try

using 1/4 tsp less yeast, substituting 1/4 cup whole-wheat flour for white flour or setting the machine on the rapid cycle (which cuts down on the rising time). If you are around and see that the rising dough is going to touch the top, quickly open the lid, prick the top of the dough with a toothpick and close the lid again; this won't give you a perfectly shaped loaf but it will help eliminate overflowing dough and a messy clean up. If the dough does touch the lid, just cut away the doughy top — the rest of the loaf will still be delicious!

Why did my loaf cave in on the sides?

In some machines the loaf will cave in if it is left in the machine after baking. Moist, tender loaves with a high percentage of butter, sugar, fruit or vegetable purées (such as Tomato-pepper, Carrot Ginger, Confetti Cheese, Double Pumpkin or Blueberry Swirl) may collapse faster than plain loaves if left in the pan, so try to remove them immediately. You might also try cutting back on the liquid slightly.

Why is the crust so hard and chewy?

Breads with decreased fat or breads that don't contain milk powder will have crispier crusts. Also, some machines have cycles designed to produce a crispier crust. To soften the crust, brush the warm loaf with melted butter or margarine after removing it from the machine, or store the loaf in a plastic bag after it cools.

Why is the top of my loaf gnarled or rough textured?

Perhaps the dough was too dry. However, many people enjoy the rough-textured crust of grain breads because it adds character to the bread. Besides, when you slice the loaf, no one knows the difference!

Why do I have doughy pockets in my loaf?

If the loaf touched the top and could not bake properly, it will have a doughy top; just cut it off and enjoy the rest of the loaf. Next time choose a smaller recipe or try reducing the amount of yeast. Also, if you chose too light a crust color, the cycle may have been too short to bake the loaf properly; next time choose a darker crust option.

Why did my loaf collapse?

Very warm or humid weather can cause the dough to rise too fast and then collapse before baking starts. If this was the case, try using colder ingredients or set the machine on the rapid cycle. The omission of salt can also cause dough to collapse. There may have been too much liquid or moisture from ingredients such as cheese, vegetables or fruit. However, you will still have a tasty loaf, even if the texture is a bit coarse.

What causes deposits of flour on the outside of the loaf?

The shape of the pan and the motion of the paddle varies from machine to machine, and sometimes the mixing and kneading action fails to incorporate all the dry ingredients from the corners. Next time, use a rubber spatula to push down any dry bits during the mixing stage.

Why does the paddle stick in the bread machine pan?

If bits of dough cool around the paddle, it will be difficult to remove. I suggest filling the pan with warm water immediately after you remove the bread and letting it soak for a few minutes. If the paddle still does not come out easily, hold the wing nut on the bottom of the pan firmly with one hand and turn the paddle back and forth with the other hand to loosen it. Keep a wooden skewer, a toothpick or a small bottle brush handy to clean out the inside of the paddle. I recommend not using soap, but if you do, rinse the pan and the paddle well, as a soapy residue will inhibit the yeast.

How can I clean the inside of the machine?

Wipe it with a damp dishcloth. To soften hard bits of food, cover with damp paper towels after the machine has cooled. An old toothbrush can also be useful.

Why does frozen bread dry out?
Bread that is not sealed completely airtight will dry out faster. Try double-wrapping the loaves with plastic wrap or foil. Wrap individual slices particularly well because they have more cut surfaces. If the cut surface of a loaf has dried out, simply cut off and dispose of a thin slice from that end — I am sure the rest will be wonderful toasted!

How can I adapt my favorite recipes to the bread machine?
You will likely have to try your recipes several times before you get successful results. Make notes of your adjustments each time. First, find a similar recipe in your manufacturer's manual or this book to use as a guideline. Then, with the help of the recipe guide on this page, adapt your recipe using quantities suggested for your machine. The trouble-shooting guide in your manual may help you to solve any problems. If you can't achieve satisfactory results baking the bread in the bread machine, make the dough in the machine, then shape by hand and bake it in the oven.

RECIPE GUIDE
Use the ratios of liquid to dry ingredients below to adapt your favorite recipes to the bread machine.

1 to 1 1/2 cups liquid*
1 to 4 tbsp fat
3/4 to 1 tsp salt
1 tsp to 3 tbsp sweetener
3 to 4 cups flour**
1 to 1 1/2 tsp bread-machine or instant yeast

*Decrease liquid by 1/4 cup for each egg in the dough. Decrease liquid by 1/2 cup for each cup of fresh vegetables or fruit. If the sweetener in the recipe is honey or molasses, count that measurement as part of the liquid.
**In Canada use all-purpose or bread flour; in the United States use bread flour. If using American rye flour, add gluten (see page 147).

index